THE HELL-HOLE IN GEORGIA

Sherman vs. Johnston
May 22-June 2, 1864

Jeffrey S. Dean

HERITAGE BOOKS
2006

HERITAGE BOOKS

AN IMPRINT OF HERITAGE BOOKS, INC.

Books, CDs, and more—Worldwide

For our listing of thousands of titles see our website
at
www.HeritageBooks.com

Published 2006 by
HERITAGE BOOKS, INC.
Publishing Division
65 East Main Street
Westminster, Maryland 21157-5026

Cover: Painting by Rick Reeves
Granbury's Texas Brigade of Cleburne's Division, C.S.A.
May 27, 1864

International Standard Book Number: 978-0-7884-3377-6

Contents

Maps

Introduction   *"No Real Battle"*

There is a class of events which by their very
nature, and despite any intrinsic interest that
they may possess, are foredoomed to oblivion. They are
merged in the general story of those greater events of
which they were a part, as the thunder of a billow
breaking on a distant beach is unnoted in the
continuous roar." [1]

In late 1863 two campaigns were enacted in
north Georgia which brought that state into
competition with Virginia for the Civil War's center
stage. The dramatic, fortuitous victory at
Chickamauga, followed two months later by the equally
celebrated Union triumph at Chattanooga, brought new
attention to the War's western theater. That focus
remains in Civil War literature today, where James
Longstreet's breakthrough and U. S. Grant's
spontaneous, unplanned assault still command the
regard of readers and historians.

However, the Atlanta Campaign has been
"merged" in the minds of most readers. There is much
more drama surrounding Lee's struggle with Grant in
Virginia or the retreat to Appomattox than is
anticipated in what William T. Sherman labeled "no
real battle, but one universal skirmish." This is
precisely why the 1864 north Georgia campaign does

not command a large audience among Civil War
enthusiasts: the battles are difficult to distinguish.
Only one of those battles encompassed the majority of
both armies, and most of them concluded with results
difficult to measure. Sherman expressed the difficulty
clearly: "It is now impossible to state accurately our loss
of life and men in any one separate battle [on the Dallas
Line]; for the fighting was continuous, almost daily,
among trees and bushes, on ground where one could
rarely see a hundred yards ahead." [2]

   This lack of attention is reflected in the War's
literature.   Only two serious studies have been
published on this event, one by a Union veteran, Jacob
Cox, in 1882.   The other, by Albert Castel, was
published more than 100 years later! Compare this to
the plethora of works on Gettysburg or Appomattox.
With so little attention focused on the Atlanta
Campaign as a whole, it should not be surprising that a
portion of this struggle should be, according to Bierce,
"foredoomed to oblivion." This study will attempt to
draw the May 1864 events on the Dallas Line from the
shadows to a status commensurate with their impact
on history.

   It was not with flippancy that the Federals
labeled the fighting at New Hope Church, Pickett's Mill,
and Dallas as the "Hell Hole." On the contrary, this
sobriquet for the struggle in Paulding County was more
than appropriate. It resulted from a change in the
character of military campaigns enacted when U. S.
Grant was placed in charge of all Federal armies.
Through a plan articulated by Grant and ratified by
Sherman, Union armies would no longer target cities or
territory; their goal would be the destruction of their
Confederate counterparts. In addition, instead of each
Northern army working independently, all United States
troops would attempt to act in concert to eliminate
Confederate military resistance.

Grant believed "that no peace could be had . . . until the military power of the rebellion was entirely broken. I therefore determined, first, to use the greatest number of troops practicable against the armed force of the enemy, preventing him from using the same force . . . against first me and then another of our armies; . . .   second, to hammer continuously against the armed force of the enemy and his resources until . . . there should be nothing left to him but an equal submission. " [3]   With this in mind, his orders to Sherman (commanding the Military Division of the Mississippi) were   "to move against [Joseph E.] Johnston's Army, to break it up, and get into the interior of the enemy's country as far as you can, inflicting all the damage you can against their war resources." Thus Grant's primary subordinate began the Atlanta Campaign on May 7 with 110,000 men, moving against Johnston's Army of 54,000 at Dalton, Georgia.[4]

Through a series of maneuvers in which Johnston's fortified lines were continuously flanked by Sherman, the two armies migrated southward to Cassville, reaching there by May 18. After a planned Confederate attack failed to materialize, a council of war held by Johnston resulted in the Army of Tennessee's further retreat on May 20 across the Etowah River   to the Allatoona Mountains. In a dispatch to President Davis on May 21, Johnston attempted to justify his retreat and alleviate Davis' disappointment: "I know that my dispatch [of May 16, reporting the retreat from Resaca] must of necessity create the feeling you express. I have earnestly sought an opportunity to strike the enemy. The direction of the railroad to this point has enabled him to press me back by steadily moving to the left and by fortifying the moment he halted. He thus made an assault upon his superior forces too hazardous." Johnston later maintained that the withdrawal was " a step which I have regretted ever since." In a letter dated May 22 to his wife, Ellen, Sherman took credit for the Confederate retreat: " we did force the Enemy to abandon the Line of the Coosa & Etowah [Rivers], which was the first Step in the Game. The next is to force him behind the Chattahoochee." 5

A Note on Army Strengths

As the Union and Confederate armies reached the Dallas Line, a substantive change had occurred in their relative strengths. Due to the need to protect critical supply points along the way, Sherman was forced to detach troops for guard duty. However, replacements and reserves had kept detachments much lower than Johnston anticipated. By the time Sherman reached New Hope Church, his troop strength was 103,000, not including the 17th Corps of the Army of the Tennessee (in transit and not yet available). Two divisions (Hovey, 23rd Corps; Baird 14th Corps), were detached at Burnt Hickory guarding supply trains, which reduced the Union Army to an effective strength of approximately 92,000. On the other hand, the Confederate Army had gathered strength as it retreated toward Atlanta, and on the Dallas Line had an approximate effective strength of 70,000. The resulting ratio of Union to Confederate strength was 1.3 to 1. Given the advantage of terrain, the Confederate Army was in a stronger position at this point in the Campaign than they had been at Dalton. 6

Chapter 1

Three Days to Dallas
"We are not idle or thoughtless"

On May 20, as the Confederate Army settled into its defenses south of the Etowah River, Sherman entered "the most valuable country above the Etowah River" and ordered a rest and re-supply for his weary army.   During this time, the Army of the Cumberland remained in the vicinity of Cassville, the Army of the Tennessee camped around Kingston, and the Army of the Ohio occupied the area near Cass Station and the previously destroyed Etowah railroad bridge. Brigadier General Jefferson C. Davis' Division (14th Army Corps) occupied Rome, GA, which had been captured on May 18.   Sherman's three armies did not have long to wait for the next stage in the campaign. Two bridges across the Etowah River, Wooley's and Gillem's, had been captured intact by Sherman's Cavalry, obviating a difficult crossing and affording Sherman the opportunity to achieve his next move.

Having traveled through the Allatoona Mountains in 1844 with the United States Army, Sherman did not expect to be able to extricate the Confederates from that stronghold. Consequently he "resolved not even to attempt it, but to turn the position, by moving from Kingston to Marietta via Dallas. " [7]   This would take the Federal Army away from its supply line for the first time in the campaign and thus required extraordinary preparations.   The

army would be expected to survive independently of the
railroad for twenty days and, for ease of movement,
must decrease their already limited baggage.   All
wounded, sick and otherwise unfit men were sent to the
rear;   rations were reduced to a minimum and orders
given for foraging off the countryside. Cavalry patrols
were strengthened and engineers made ready for the
move.[8] Sherman's orders for May 22 directed that the
move to bypass the Confederate Army in the Allatoona
Mountains should begin the next day with the crossing
of the Etowah River.   The Army of the Cumberland
would move south to Dallas via the tiny settlements of
Euharlee and Stilesboro, while Davis' Division at Rome
would be replaced by other troops   and proceed to
Dallas through Van Wert.[9]   McPherson's Army was to
have the longest march, moving southwest to Van Wert
and approaching Dallas from the west. The Army of the
Ohio received the task of protecting the Federal left
flank, closest to the Confederates at Allatoona.   The
17th Corps, commanded by Major General Frank Blair,
was directed to move from Decatur, Alabama, via Rome
to Kingston, there to remain in reserve until called
forward.   Sherman's expectations for this operation
were expressed in a telegram dated May 21 to Henry W.
Halleck, Army Chief of Staff: "I allow three days to have
the army grouped about Dallas, whence I can strike
Marietta,   or   the   Chattahoochee,   according   to
developments. You may not hear from us in some days,
but be assured we are not idle or thoughtless." [10]
Gathering his forces around Dallas would prove
achievable for the Union commander, as would avoiding
a confrontation at Allatoona. Getting into Marietta was
another matter, however, and depended upon the
Confederates' reaction.   Joe Johnston was not idle
during this time either, and had his own expectations.

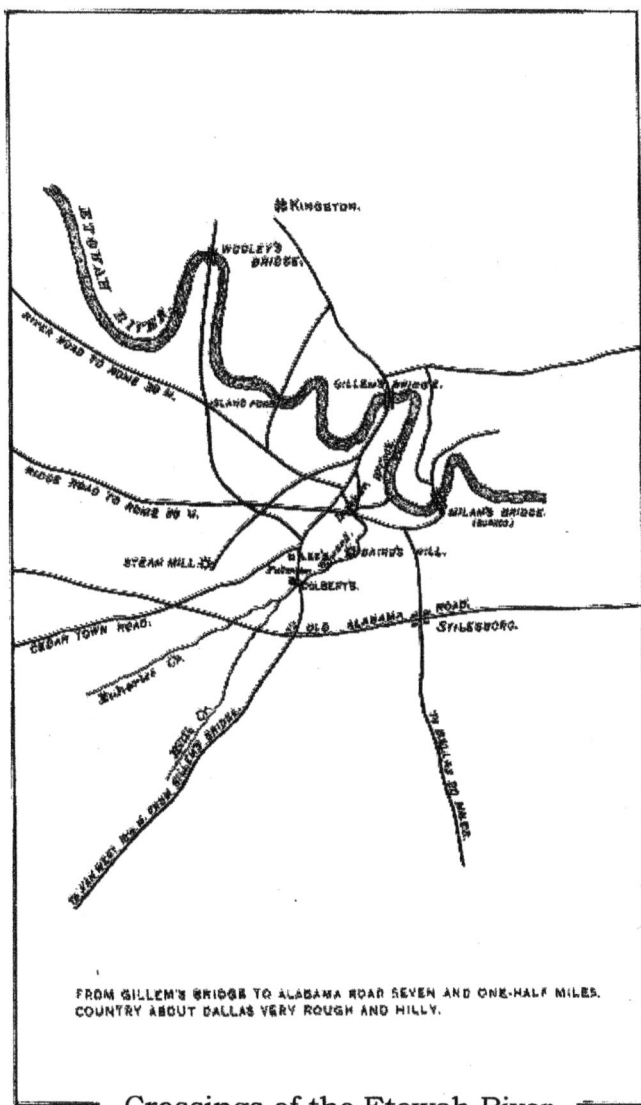

FROM GILLEM'S BRIDGE TO ALABAMA ROAD SEVEN AND ONE-HALF MILES.
COUNTRY ABOUT DALLAS VERY ROUGH AND HILLY.

Crossings of the Etowah River

Sherman's plans to cross the Etowah involved consideration of the limited number of roads available, as well as the river's few bridges and steep banks. Major General George Thomas' Army, occupying the center of the movement, used Gillem's Bridge and Island Ford, downstream from the bridge. The 20th Corps, commanded by Major General Joseph Hooker, was ordered to march at 4 a.m. on May 23 from Cassville to Gillem's, then encamp on the south bank of the Etowah along Euharlee Creek. Four hours later, Major General O. O. Howard's 4th Corps would start, following the same route as Hooker's men, ending their day along Euharlee Creek, but upstream from Hooker. Using a different road, the First Cavalry Division (Brigadier General Edward McCook) was also ordered to start at 4 a.m., cross the Etowah at Island Ford, and camp below the 20th Corps. From that point they were to send out an advance guard to Stilesboro and along all other roads to the south and east, protecting the crossing from Confederate attack. Following McCook at 8 a.m., the 14th Corps (commanded by Major General John M. Palmer) was to cross and stop on Euharlee Creek, above the 4th Corps.[11]   Major General John M. Schofield's Army of the Ohio, camped farthest to the east before the move, was ordered to cross the Etowah east (upstream) of Thomas and serve as the army's left-flank guard. Having no bridge in the assigned crossing area, Schofield requested a pontoon bridge from Sherman, which was supplied. The bridge was laid near Shellman's Ford in the vicinity of the Etowah Cliffs. Orders were given to Army of the Ohio commanders to begin marching at 6 a.m.; they were expected to reach the river bridge by noon. Major General George Stoneman, commander of the Army of the Ohio's cavalry, was ordered to guard the wagon trains in their transit across the river, then to follow them to the south bank and cover the left flank of the army. [12]

The Army of the Tennessee, meanwhile, was ordered by McPherson to begin the river crossing at 5 a.m. with the cavalry (under Brigadier General Kenner Garrard) using Gillem's Bridge, the same as that used by McCook's cavalry. The 15th Corps, commanded by Major General John Logan, would move next, at 6 a.m., and cross using Wooley's Bridge. They would continue beyond the bridge along the Van Wert Road. [13] Major General Grenville Dodge's Corps, the 16th, was ordered to follow Logan, using the same route. [14] In a message sent to Nashville on May 23, Sherman thanked Colonel Donaldson for the gift of a horse and expressed his excitement about the crossing: "Horse arrived . . . I will ride him to-morrow across the Etowah, which is the Rubicon of Georgia. We are now all in motion like a vast hive of bees, and expect to swarm along the Chattahoochee in five days."[15] The Federal commander's optimism, however, would not engender success, and the swarming would be delayed until the first week of July, more than a month away.

Carrying a large army over a river with limited crossing-points was not accomplished without problems. The most significant of these arose when Schofield's troops reached the pontoon bridge over the river around noon: Hooker's 20th Corps was already using the bridge. Rather than cause a delay, Schofield decided to wait for Hooker to cross, and did not complete his crossing until the next day. The problem was caused by Sherman's assumption that Schofield would cross the Etowah farther upstream from Etowah Cliffs, near the mouth of Pettit's Creek. When congestion developed downstream at Gillem's Bridge, Sherman attempted to rectify the situation by ordering Hooker to cross his Corps at a ford upstream. Unfortunately, this was the same area where, apparently unknown to Sherman, Schofield had placed his pontoon bridge! As he explained later, Schofield did not interfere with Hooker's crossing because he knew Sherman wanted Thomas' larger army across the river first. [16]

McCook's Cavalry, having crossed at Island Ford, moved east and encountered Brigadier General William Jackson's Confederate Cavalry at Stilesboro. In a brief engagement the Confederates were forced to retreat, allowing McCook to secure the Union Army's left flank south of the river. [17]

Thus, by the evening of May 23, the Federals (less the Army of the Ohio) had crossed a major obstacle in the campaign without significant opposition from the Confederates. "It was an excellent day's work, to get these columns well over the river," commented Captain Henry Stone, "with so few bridges, . . . and the banks so steep and rocky that few places were available for pontoons." [18]

Sherman had another reason to be happy: he would not have to fight the Confederates at Allatoona. One Federal soldier, having crossed the Etowah River, made an appropriate observation: "For our lives we could not imagine any cause why we were brought away around this way leaving our 'base' so exposed, for it seemed reasonable that the rebs would subsist as well away from their base of operations as we could from ours, and it also seemed reasonable that if we went around them to capture Atlanta that they would go around us and take Chattanooga. But the result proved that 'Billy' understood flanking, at least, a little better than us." [19]

The Confederate commander had deployed his cavalry to watch the river crossings: Major General Joseph Wheeler's Corps upstream from the Etowah River railroad bridge and Jackson's below it. The remainder of the Army of Tennessee was deployed in the vicinity of Allatoona, along the Etowah River to the north and Pumpkinvine Creek to the west. [20]   As early as May 21st, Johnston received a report from Jackson of Federal concentration along the Etowah near Wooley's Bridge.   By the 23rd it was obvious to Johnston that a major enemy crossing was occurring in that area, so he immediately gave orders to begin the transfer of his Army to the southwest. Hardee's and Polk's Corps were ordered to move, beginning on the morning of the 23rd, in the direction of Dallas. Hood's Corps remained at Allatoona to cover the railroad crossing. [21]   Meanwhile, to gain further information, Wheeler was ordered to cross to the north side of the Etowah and reconnoiter toward the enemy.   The Confederate cavalry not needed for river patrol crossed at night on May 23 and the next night attacked the Federal wagon train at Cass Station.   Here they encountered Federal cavalry and infantry guarding the train but, despite the opposition, managed to capture or destroy 100 wagons. [22]   By May 24, Johnston was convinced that his position at Allatoona was untenable. He declined to strongly contest Sherman's crossing and ordered Hood's Corps to follow Hardee's along the road to Dallas. This decision was unwise, even though it fit Johnston's plan of not risking his Army until the enemy had been lured to the outskirts of Atlanta.   Given the advantage he had in the terrain, Johnston could have produced a better defense of the Etowah, including the destruction of all the bridges. Allowing Sherman an easy river crossing would be repeated by Johnston later in the Campaign in a similar scenario on the Chattahoochee River, where it would cost the Confederate Commander his job. [23]

Chapter 2

Coming to Grips
"Marching on by division front"

Early on the morning of May 24, Sherman's Army was gathered around the junction of Euharlee Creek and the Etowah River, with orders to concentrate on Dallas, twenty miles to the south. McCook's cavalry had already encountered the Confederates at Stilesboro, but no other enemy had been contacted. Thomas ordered Hooker's 20th Corps to lead the Army of the Cumberland for the day. In order to prevent enemy incursions, Brigadier General John Geary's Division was sent east toward Raccoon Creek and Stilesboro to screen the march route of Brigadier General Alpheus Williams' and Major General Daniel Butterfield's Divisions. Geary would be relieved by Schofield's troops after their crossing of the River. The Army of the Cumberland's movements were to be covered by McCook's cavalry.

Following Hooker were the 4th and 14th Corps, on a road parallel and west of that taken by the 20th Corps. All the routes from Stilesboro to Dallas joined at a crossroads called Burnt Hickory, or Huntsville, where a post office was located. This was the next concentration point for the Army of the Cumberland. 24

Brigadier General Milo Hascall's and Brigadier General Jacob Cox's Divisions of Schofield's Army

finally succeeded in crossing the Etowah at the pontoon
bridge used by Hooker the day before. After relieving
Geary's Division of Thomas' Army, they proceeded east
across Raccoon Creek and then along roads running
southeast, parallel to Richland Creek and through
Sligh's Mill. Hascall and Cox were followed by Brigadier
General Alvin Hovey's Division, following the same
route. [25]

The Army of the Tennessee, less the 17th Corps,
began its May 24 march by taking the road southwest
from the Etowah camp to Van Wert. They were joined
enroute by Davis' Division (14th Corps) from Rome,
which followed them for a while before finding a less-
congested road east toward Dallas. The 17th Corps
was under orders to move up, but by May 23, had only
reached Huntsville, Alabama. [26]

When Sherman's men left the Etowah and moved
south toward Dallas, they entered a region of Georgia
described by many as a wilderness. One such
description comes from Henry Stone: "Immediately
below Euharlee Creek, the character of the country
again changes, and it becomes ever more hilly, rocky,
and wooded. Indeed, from Burnt Hickory, about twelve
miles south of the Etowah, an almost unbroken forest
stretches east to the railroad and south to the
Chattahoochee, with here and there a clearing, cut up
with numerous streams, and scanty dirt roads. The
Wilderness in Virginia cannot be blinder." [27]

Chesley Mosman, a Lieutenant in the 59th
Illinois (4th Corps), began his May 24th march with at
8 a.m. His experience is typical of many soldiers
marching through this region that day: "Went south
and kept going to any point of compass from NW to NE,
winding in every direction. Halted for ten times.
Struck a mountainous country. Went up a mountain
road. That's the last that I could see to tell about. . . .
Woods are so thick we went in one rank [marching

along roadside]. Rain in torrents and blinding flashes
of lightning and we got on the road. Teams [of wagons]
in it. . . . Lost our commander so we camp ourselves,
letting anybody pass as wanted to. . . . Distance
traveled - 20 miles, around 10 miles south. It seems
the whole army was marching on by division front." [28]
Another Federal soldier, however, had a more optimistic
view: "I hardly think we will have another big fight this
side of Atlanta, which place we expect to occupy June
1st. . . . We passed through the finest country I have
yet seen in Dixie, this morning. Splendid farms,
spacious mansions. . . . A sesech lady had the kindness
to give me a canteen of molasses today as we passed
her house. It goes nice on hardtack." [29]

    As the Federals moved south, contact with the
Confederates came at several points. One of the most
significant occurred while approaching Burnt Hickory,
when a Confederate courier was captured. He was
carrying orders to the Confederate cavalry commander
at that point (Jackson), giving information regarding
Sherman's movements and advising Jackson that
Confederate troops were enroute to Dallas. Another
clash came west of Dallas, where Garrard's cavalry was
screening McPherson's advance. Here Colonel Robert
Minty's Brigade and infantry of the 15th Corps were
attacked by troops of Major General William Bate's
Division, Hardee's Corps. These encounters made
Sherman aware that Confederate troops had not been
deceived by the Federal flanking move, and were in
close proximity. The day ended with the Federal Army
camped in the wilderness south of the Etowah: The
Army of the Cumberland near Burnt Hickory, the Army
of the Ohio around Sligh's Mill to the northeast, and
McPherson's Army between Van Wert and Dallas. [30]

    While Sherman's Army struggled through the
rough country of Paulding County, the Army of
Tennessee continued its shift to the southwest,

maintaining contact with the Federals. Hardee was already enroute to Dallas, as was Polk's Corps on a parallel road to the east. Major General Patrick Cleburne's Division, leaving the vicinity of Williford's Mill (on Pumpkinvine Creek), marched six miles toward Dallas and camped. The next morning Cleburne moved through New Hope Church to Powder Springs, about 10 miles southeast of Dallas. On the morning of May 24, Hardee had reached the Robertson House, five miles east of Dallas, where he sent a message to Polk, then in the vicinity of Lost Mountain. [31]

Hood's Corps had followed Hardee to Dallas also, and by the night of May 24, was four miles northeast of New Hope Church, at Dr. Smith's house. While enroute, early on May 24, Bate's Division of Hardee's Corps was ordered to halt at New Hope Church and reinforce Jackson's cavalry patrolling near Dallas. Brigadier General Thomas Smith's Brigade and one section of artillery was sent to the cavalry's aid, where they encountered Minty's troopers. An additional force (two regiments of Finley's Florida Brigade, commanded by Colonel Robert Bullock) was sent from Bate to strengthen the Confederate presence there. [32] This clash caused Johnston, late in the day, to order Hardee west from Powder Springs to Dallas, and Polk from Lost Mountain to Robertson's House. [33] Johnston thus effectively blocked Sherman's path to Marietta by concentrating along a line running from north of New Hope Church to Dallas. May 24th closed with a rough night in the rain for those Confederates camped near Dallas: one soldier "slept on three fence-rails placed side-by-side, one end of the rails resting up against the fence, to give inclination, so the water would run off." [34]

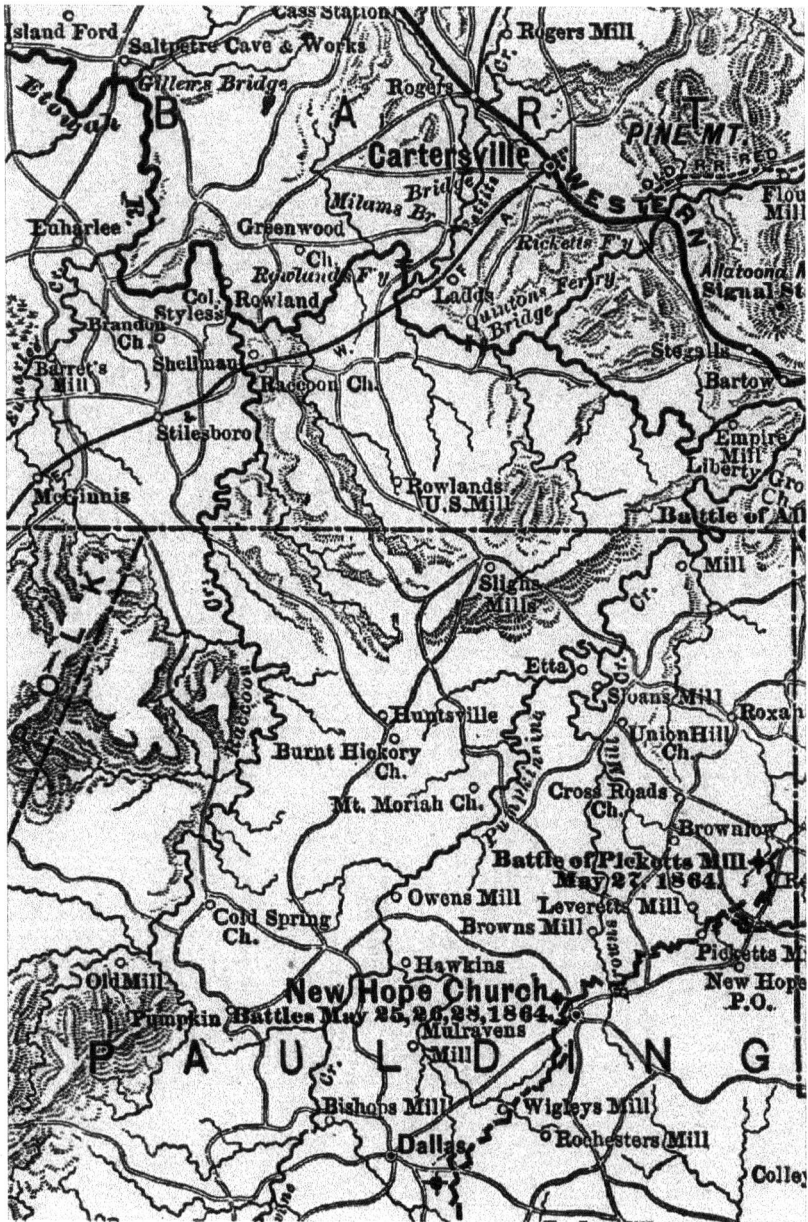

Campaign Area

May 25 was "showery all day, and the weather and bad roads had a disheartening effect on men and animals." [35]   Despite this, Sherman continued his move to Dallas with all three of his armies.   McPherson's Army of the Tennessee, led by the 15th Corps, left its camp on the headwaters of Raccoon Creek (west of Dallas) at 7 a.m. and moved east toward Dallas on the Van Wert Road.[36]   They were preceded by Garrard's Cavalry Division, which had already encountered Confederate resistance at Pumpkinvine Creek.   The 15th Corps march was led by Brigadier General William Harrow's Division, followed by Brigadier General Peter Osterhaus' and Brigadier General Morgan Smith's. Dodge's 16th Corps followed Logan's Corps, but would not reach Pumpkinvine Creek until that night. [37]

To the northwest, Schofield attempted to hold the Union left, but had difficulty due to the limited number of roads. Beginning the day at Sligh's Mill, the Army of the Ohio moved rapidly enough through Burnt Hickory, but then ran into the 20th and 4th Corps traveling on the main road to Dallas. In this area both Hascall's and Cox's divisions stopped and were unable to proceed further that day. Later in the day, when Hascall received orders to support Hooker at New Hope Church, he was unable to comply. Hovey's Division remained around Burnt Hickory, guarding wagon trains, until May 28. [38]

Thomas' Army struggled southward from the Burnt Hickory vicinity, using all roads available. McCook's Division pushed forward on a road east of the main road to Dallas, leading Butterfield's Division (20th Corps) across Pumpkinvine Creek. In this vicinity McCook observed Confederate troops (reported as Stevenson's Division), moving along the Dallas-Allatoona Road (running through New Hope Church).

The Federals' reconnaissance efforts were limited, however, by a heavy Confederate cavalry screen.[39]

Geary's Division (20th Corps) marched on the Dallas-Burnt Hickory road, with Williams' Division moving on a parallel road to the west. These roads were also used by the 14th Army Corps, following Hooker's troops. [40]   Unaware of the proximity of Confederate troops, Thomas intended that Butterfield's Division would gain possession of the Dallas-Allatoona Road near New Hope Church, while Williams' and Geary's Divisions would move through Dallas, reach the Dallas-Marietta Road, and connect with Butterfield's right. The 4th and 14th Corps would move on Dallas and support the 20th. However, as Geary's Division proceeded south from Burnt Hickory toward Dallas, they were attacked from the east at Owen's Mill, forcing Thomas to quickly re-evaluate his objectives.

On the morning of May 25th, Johnston focused on blocking of the Federal's advance to Dallas. He therefore ordered Hood to deploy his troops at New Hope Church, and directed Polk's Corps to Hood's left. Hardee's divisions were ordered to form on the left of Polk, and hold the Dallas-Marietta road. [41]   Hood arrived at New Hope Church around 10 a.m., and having received reports of Federal movements to the west, ordered   Brigadier General Henry Clayton (Stewart's Division) to reconnoiter up the road from the road junction to Owen's Mill. Clayton selected Colonel Bushrod Jones' 32nd/58th Alabama, which moved immediately. They arrived in the vicinity of Owen's Mill, where Colonel Dudley Jones' 9th Texas Cavalry were already in contact with Federal cavalry. Under orders to develop the enemy's strength, the Confederate infantry pushed forward.[42]

Chapter 3   The Battle of New Hope Church
"There haven't been twenty rebels there today"

The Battle of New Hope Church is essentially a two-phase conflict, the first phase involving the initial confrontation at Owen's Mill bridge and ensuing combat in that area. A lull then occurred as the Federal advance was halted and reinforced, while the Confederates fell back on their supporting troops nearby. When additional Union troops arrived, they were moved forward to begin phase two, the main assault in the vicinity of the Church.

On the high ground east of Owen's Mill, the Confederate force sent forward by Hood quickly encountered stiff Federal infantry resistance, forcing the reconnaissance force to assume the defensive about 1 p.m. However, they were soon reinforced by Brigadier General Randall Gibson's Brigade from Stewart's Division, the 19th Louisiana and Austin's Battalion (also known as the 14th Louisiana Battalion) arriving first. [43]   Their arrival changed the posture of the Confederate force, and precipitated a general engagement. Confederates soon learned from captured prisoners that they faced Geary's Division.

Geary had reached this spot by taking a wrong turn, thinking he was on the main road to Dallas. He had arrived around 9 a.m. at the Owen's Mill bridge in the company of Thomas and Hooker, and found Jones' Texas cavalry setting fire to it. Hooker's headquarters escort was promptly ordered to chase the enemy away and seize the bridge, which they accomplished. After Geary's pioneers repaired the bridge, the 7th Ohio (Colonel Charles Candy's Brigade) led the Division across. When strong Confederate resistance was encountered on the opposite side, the 29th Pennsylvania was ordered to reinforce the 7th Ohio on the skirmish line. After pushing forward 1 1/2 miles "through the thick underbrush . . . where one could not see the length of a company . . . against a steadily increasing storm of bullets," the Federal advance was halted by B. Jones' and Gibsons' brigades.

Colonel Jones sent a message to General Stewart regarding the increasing Federal pressure, and was told to hold his position. Since Jones "thought the best means of holding it was to meet an attack by a counter attack," he ordered his troops forward: the 32nd/58th Alabama along the road and Austin's Battalion on his left. Candy's Federals managed to repulse this attack and then, with the support of Geary's remaining brigades, continued the advance. They soon flanked both ends of Jones' line, forcing the Confederates to retreat "barely in time to escape the capture of the entire regiment [32nd/58th Alabama]." [44]

However, the fierce Confederate resistance coupled with information received from captured prisoners that Hood's whole Corps was ahead, caused Geary to halt the advance. Geary, Thomas, and Hooker, all on the scene at the time, "felt extreme anxiety at the unexpected development." Geary's assessment gives the clearest picture: "My division was isolated, at least five miles from the nearest supporting troops [Williams' and Butterfield's Divisions], and had been sustaining a sharp conflict with the enemy for four hours. Close in my front was an *overwhelming* force."

Henry Stone relates this incident: "As the enemy's fire was increasing, General Thomas ordered me, almost in a whisper, to ride back to [O.O.] Howard as fast as I could, and hurry up the 4th Corps. . . . As I was starting off briskly, he called me back and cautioned me to walk my horse till I was out of sight of the troops. As I left him there was a sudden outburst of musketry, . . . which filled me with dread that the enemy had discovered our *weakness*, and was closing down on the solitary Division with *overwhelming* strength." While reinforcements were being ordered forward, Geary ordered his men to "keep up an aggressive fire. . . to deceive the enemy as to our *weakness* by a show of strength."[45] (emphasis added)   Colonel Jones' aggressive tactics had intimidated a superior force, accomplishing exactly what the Confederates needed at this time.

Moving southeast from Burnt Hickory, Dan Butterfield's Division was the first Union reinforcement to arrive; it reached the Pumpkinvine Creek bridge about 2 p.m. McCook's cavalry had already crossed and were skirmishing with the Confederates. Due to the use of the same road by McCook, the infantry's advance had been slow. Butterfield finally reached the junction with the Owen's Mill-New Hope Church road around 3 p.m., where they found Geary on the defensive, in close contact with the Confederates.[46]

Farther to the rear, a message carried by Lieutenant Colonel John Mendenhall finally reached the 4th Corps Headquarters in the early afternoon. The headquarters was located at the Harding House, on the road between Burnt Hickory and Dallas, the same road that Williams' Division had used earlier. Howard was ordered immediately to press on to Hooker's aid. Later, as they proceeded toward Owen's Mill, they met Henry Stone with his urgent message from Thomas. Howard replied that he was on his way as fast as possible.[47]

About 2 p.m., the order reached Williams (2nd) Division directing him to support Geary. At the time, Williams was on the Burnt Hickory-Dallas Road within 1 1/2 miles of Dallas. He had left Burnt Hickory that morning, using a road west of Geary's route, and reached the burned-out bridge over Pumpkinvine Creek southeast of Owen's Mill. After a delay while the bridge was rebuilt, Williams proceeded south toward Dallas. Upon receipt of the order from Thomas, the Federals immediately counter-marched across Pumpkinvine Creek, then up the west bank of the stream to the Owen's Mill bridge. Here they also encountered Stone, who was returning from Howard's Headquarters after delivering his message. Moving along the road to New Hope Church, Williams encountered Geary's and Butterfield's (3rd) divisions massed along the road. Under orders from Hooker, Williams then moved his Division to the front, on Geary's right. Sergeant Rice Bull, of Williams' Division, recorded the scene as they marched: "As we neared the front there were all the evidences of battle, wounded men being brought back, ammo. wagons and ambulances hurrying to the front, cowardly skulkers . . . getting to the rear, men, horses, and even mules wild with excitement." [48]

While these movements were in progress General Sherman, in the vicinity of Owen's Mill, met Captain Stone returning to Thomas. Stone advised the Federal commander that Williams' Division would soon be up. Sherman then added a few words on the back of a message just received from McPherson: "Let Williams go in anywhere as soon as he gets up. I don't see what they are waiting for in front now. There haven't been 20 rebels there to-day." Stone was directed to forward McPherson's message along with the note inscribed to Thomas without delay.[49] The Army of the Cumberland commander undoubtedly read the message with consternation; he had dealt with many more than twenty of Hood's men. While the Union commander's agressiveness was an asset in most of the situations he faced; Thomas would soon find the opposite to be true at New Hope Church.

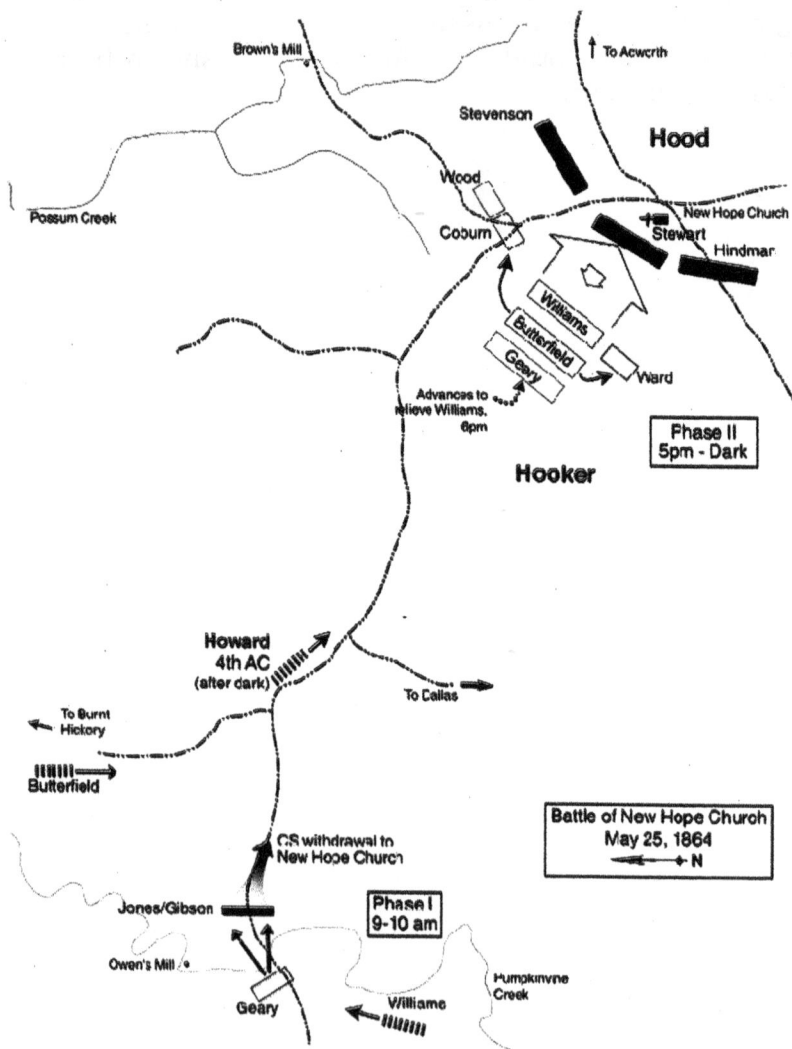

Brown's Mill

To Acworth

Stevenson

Hood

Wood

Possum Creek

New Hope Church

Coburn

Stewart

Hindman

Williams

Butterfield

Geary

Ward

Advances to
relieve Williams.
6pm

Phase II
5pm - Dark

Hooker

Howard
4th AC
(after dark)

To Callas

To Burnt
Hickory

Butterfield

Battle of New Hope Church
May 25, 1864
N

CS withdrawal to
New Hope Church

Phase I
9-10 am

Jones/Gibson

Owen's Mill

Pumpkinvine
Creek

Geary

Williams

Chapter 4   New Hope Church, Phase Two
"A storm of canister and shrapnel"

The situation on the front line had changed significantly since Geary had driven the Confederates from their last position near the New Hope-Burnt Hickory road junction. Having accomplished their reconnaissance mission, these troops had been ordered to withdraw to Hood's main line at New Hope Church, about two miles to the rear. This position was configured with Major General Thomas Hindman's Division southeast of the Church, followed on the right by Major General Alexander Stewart's Division closest to the Church and road junction. Stewart's three brigades (Stovall, Clayton, Baker) were deployed left to right on the front line. The 18th Alabama was placed on the skirmish line. On Stewart's right was Major General Carter Stevenson's Division with Brown and Pettus on the front line; Cumming and Reynolds in reserve. Eldridge's Battalion of artillery, consisting of Stanford's, Oliver's and Fenner's Batteries, 16 guns in all, was well-positioned behind the infantry.[50]   Austin's Battalion withdrew from its advanced position in Geary's front to act as skirmishers for Stewart's Division. Gibson's Brigade also retreated to the main line and was placed in reserve. The 32nd/58th Alabama withdrew to a reserve position behind Clayton's line.[51]

Several factors now combined to initiate phase two of this battle. The Confederate withdrawal, following on the heels of the Federal concentration, indicated to the Union commanders a weak enemy, exactly what might be expected in a delaying action. Thomas' initial fears were ameliorated with the breaking of enemy resistance, perhaps leading to a desire to take advantage of the situation by pushing forward. Victories had often been gained by a rapid advance on a retreating force. Thomas may have begun to see things as Sherman did: a few rebels making a lot of trouble. Sherman was not going to leave the action in Thomas' hands, however; Williams' division had already been ordered to the front.

When the forward elements of the Union advance developed the main Confederate position, Hooker's Corps was arranged for the assault: each division in column of brigades, Williams first, followed by Butterfield, then Geary. All three units were aligned to the right (south) of the Owen's Mill-New Hope Church Road.[52] The column-of-brigades formation allowed the commanders better control in the woods and also gave the attackers more power at the point of attack. It's great disadvantage, however, was that the narrow front offered the defender ample opportunities for enfilade fire. New Hope Church would be the Campaign's debut of this attack formation; and would see a reprise two days later at Pickett's Mill.

About 5 p.m., the Federals began their advance. Williams' Division was led by Colonel James Robinson's (3rd) Brigade, followed by Brigadier General Thomas Ruger's (2nd), then Brigadier General Joseph Knipe's (1st). Two regiments (61st Ohio, 13th New Jersey) were thrown forward in front of Robinson. General Williams positioned himself just behind the first battleline, and observed his soldiers as they advanced "in beautiful order." This was not the case for long, however, as the assault rapidly disintegrated into chaos. The skirmishers soon clashed with their Confederate counterparts, who were driven back onto their advanced supports, causing increased resistance to the Federal push.   Williams responded by ordering a "double-quick" march, forcing a rapid Confederate retreat, and bringing the Union advance in range of the Confederate artillery on the main line. At this point, a storm of canister and shrapnel engulfed the Federals "from all directions except the rear."   General Geary later reported that the Confederate artillery fire was "heavier than in any other battle of the campaign in which my command were engaged." [53]

On the Confederate side, a member of Stanford's Mississippi Battery recounted this assault: "Batteries take position on line with the infantry, while the skirmishers are being driven in. They are close by followed by heavy lines of Yankee infantry, charging our lines, firing as they come, yelling through the bushes, which are so dense that we cannot see the enemy, though distant only from 200 . . . yards from us. . . . Our company's loss had been so great that we could work but two guns." [54]   This devastating barrage quickly thinned the attacking Federal ranks: Robinson was relieved by Ruger's Brigade on the front line, and Knipe's Brigade moved up to the right of and behind Ruger. A soldier of the 3rd Wisconsin described Ruger's attack: "The country was heavily timbered, and underbrush so obscured the view that it was impossible to see in any direction more than a few rods. When we came within sight of the enemy, we found that a 6-gun battery was posted a little in front of their line of infantry. . . . As soon as we came within range, the battery opened on us with round shot and shell; then, as we came nearer, with grape and canister. But we pushed steadily on until we were less than 60 yards from them, when he halted; for we had lost so many men, and had become so disorganized in the march through the timber and brush that the impetus of our charge was gone. . . . We succeeded however, in driving off the Confederate gunners, and prevented the cannon from being worked for the remainder of the day." [55]

As the Union attack followed the road's curve to the southeast, Hooker's men began to receive flank fire from their left. Led by Colonel James Wood's Brigade (3rd), followed by Colonel John Coburn's (2nd) and Brigadier General William Ward's (1st), Butterfield's Division (in rear of Williams) was quickly moved up to assist the beleaguered Federals. Moving to Williams' left, a soldier of the 73rd Ohio (Wood's Brigade) recorded the action: "True, it seemed like madness for a single regiment, without connections right or left, to move upon an extended line of the enemy, when that line was protected by temporary breastworks; but the order was preemptory, and must be obeyed." [56] Despite his trepidation, the 73rd Ohio was not alone, but was accompanied by other units of Wood's Brigade as they attempted to protect Williams' left flank. Coburn moved directly ahead to relieve Knipe's depleted brigade near the road. Led by the 19th Michigan and 33rd Indiana, these troops began trading fire with the enemy in their front, and, according to Coburn, were able to silence the musketry from Stevenson's Confederates, but not before both these units had suffered a heavy punishment in their own ranks, as "shells, grape-shot, canister, railroad spikes, and every deadly missile rained around [them]." Coburn commended their gallantry with these words: ". . . no regiment could have borne with more unfaltering daring this fearful cannonade and musketry fire than did the Thirty-third Indiana that day. So, too, with the Nineteenth Michigan." [57]

The last brigade in Butterfield's assault column, Ward's, was ordered to Williams' right in an attempt to attack the Confederate left flank. Marching at the double-quick, Ward first arrived behind some of

Coburn's units where their "line, with one involuntary movement, was swayed for an instant towards the earth - like a field of wheat in a storm - as the screeching shells swept overhead." [58]   Shifting farther to the right to avoid this artillery fire, Ward finally arrived at the desired location.   However, his brigade had gotten divided in the movement through the thick woods, and only one regiment (79th Ohio) stood ready to make the attack. Although Ward sent many couriers back to find his "lost" regiments, the remainder of his unit never arrived before darkness set in and the assault was canceled.[59]

After an hour of punishment from Confederate artillery and musketry, the impetus of the Federal assault was drained. Geary's Division, which during this time was in rear of Williams, received orders to move to the front. As darkness approached, Geary's men moved forward and received the same effect as their predecessors.   Colonel George Cobham's and Candy's brigades went into the teeth of the Confederate fire, for Candy the second serious engagement of the day. Two regiments of Coburn, the 111th Pennsylvania and 149th New York, actually attempted to capture one of the lethal Confederate batteries, but "the terrible discharges of grape and canister. . . literally swept [the Federals] away." [60]

As darkness finally arrived to cover the carnage and diminish the fighting, a thunderstorm struck. While many previous accounts of this battle depict the storm coming at the height of the fighting, it seems clear from the Federal accounts that the rain came as the battle ceased and night fell. Evidence of this comes from the report of the 33rd Indiana (Coburn's Brigade, Butterfield's Division): "About dusk I ordered my men to cease firing and lie down. . . . About this time it commenced to rain and continued a cold, wet rain for about two and a half hours." Another report from

Wood's Brigade (Butterfield's Division) should suffice to prove the point: "With the close of day a rain-storm and intense darkness set in, which put a stop to operations on both sides." [61] Despite the effect of the rain on their desperate plight, another account reflects a soldier's typical asperity. As with the 33rd Indiana, this Union unit had been ordered to lie down: "while lying there a thunder shower that had threatened all day broke on us. It was a furious storm, the rain came down in torrents, the lightning was blinding; then the darkness so black it could almost be felt. . . . During the storm one of the boys, who was quite a wag, lying in a pool of water turned to Captain Anderson (123 NY) . . . and said, 'Now Captain, if you will just give the order, we will swim over and tackle the Johnnies.'" [62]

Darkness allowed the Union forces time to measure their losses, although under the circumstances this task was daunting. General Howard described the Federal situation that evening: "The nearest house to the field was filled with the wounded. Torch-lights and candles lighted up dimly the incoming stretchers and the surgeon's table and instruments. The very woods seemed to moan and groan with the voices of sufferers not yet brought in." [63] A courier of Howard's Corps remembered that night: "I encountered many a dead soldier. I could not see them for the pitchy darkness, but my horse when he came to one would shy and go around them." While the dead and wounded were tallied, the survivors attempted to rest. Their efforts, however, were often unsuccessful, due to the nervousness reigning on the front lines. One soldier found a safe sleeping spot on the ground behind a log which protected him from Confederate fire. However, just after he had settled down to a well-deserved rest, a picket nearby fired at a suspected movement in the woods, causing other Union soldiers to add their share. The result was typical: "The rebels thinking a night attack was on foot opened fire from behind their works . . . not five hundred yards distant from our line. . . . our men thinking the rebs were coming, opened fire from the batteries, and the infantry poured in their lead; all the rattle of ten thousand rifles and fifty cannon, made a pandemonium of sound. . . . For the thirty minutes it lasted the air was pretty well filled with lead and iron. It finally dawned on the enemy, and our men, that there was not going to be any assault from either side; firing ceased, almost as suddenly as it commenced, when quiet reigned again."[64]

At another point along the line on the Confederate side, another night action ensued involving Brigadier General Francis Cockrell's Brigade (French's Division, Polk's Corps): "Just what started it, no one seemed to know. . . . For several minutes there prevailed all the concomitants of a pitched battle, only neither army advanced. Everybody was shooting but Cockrell's men. Up to these rode an irate colonel of another command. 'What troops are these? Why in hell aren't you shooting?,' he demanded." A private quickly stepped forward and informed the colonel that this was Cockrell's Brigade, and that their skirmishers were still out in front. "Just then the firing ceased, and the abashed colonel returned to his own command." [65]

Federal casualties, as reported by Hooker, were 1665, with Williams' Division taking the worst punishment: 805. Butterfield's and Geary's Divisions suffered casualties of 418 and 376 respectively.[66] Confederate losses were not nearly as severe: about 450. According to General Stewart, this was due primarily to the Federal's shooting high, over the heads of the Confederates. To a lesser degree it was also caused by the "few logs" piled up in front of Baker's and Clayton's brigades; Stovall's Brigade had no protection.

The intense Confederate artillery fire and the resulting Federal concentration on the cannons caused heavy casualties in Eldridge's battalion: 43 men and 44 horses.[67]

Once the fighting diminished to occasional shooting, the Federals began digging in, using any tools available.   As was often the case in the Atlanta Campaign, digging tools were carried by mules, which, unlike wagons, could be brought through the thick woods with their life-saving implements.[68]

The reinforcements that Thomas had ordered earlier (the 4th and 14th Corps) were just now arriving, a trifle late.   A soldier in Howard's Corps recalled a typical experience as they moved to the front: "Just enough rain had fallen to make the hard beaten road slippery, and we found great difficulty in ascending the hill from the creek (Pumpkinvine).   We then advanced by slow degrees a few miles further, and after being almost wearied to death by continual standing we were finally (about 10 o'clock p.m.) ordered to bivouac by the roadside just in the order in which we had marched" [69] Another scene witnessed along the roadside that night was of General Sherman, who sat upon a log "cheery and undisturbed, as if the most ordinary business were going on, . . . and sketched upon a leaf of his pocket memorandum book a map . . . for the use of the officer leading the [reinforcement] column.   Its firm delicate lines, and neat touches, even to the fine lettering of the names of houses and roads, showed how completely his nerves were unaffected by the night of battle and storm." General Schofield was not so unaffected, as his horse fell into a ditch during the night march to the front and injured him, seriously enough to force a temporary abdication of his command in favor of General Jacob Cox.[70]

Despite the evidence to the contrary, Sherman maintained his opinion that the delay at Owen's Mill had cost him a "splendid opportunity". During the Battle, this belief was reflected in his note to Thomas carried by Captain Stone (see page 25). On June 18, in a letter to Grant, Sherman blamed the loss at New Hope on the "Slowness" of the Army of the Cumberland: "At Dallas there was a delay of four hours to get ready to advance, when we first met Johnston's head of Column, and that four hours enabled him to throw up works to cover the head of his column and he extended the work about as fast as we deployed." This statement refers to the halt by Geary's Division after crossing Pumpkinvine Creek, and receiving the attack by Jones. Thomas and Hooker at that point did not know the strength of the enemy facing them, and, based on the Confederates' aggressiveness, took the prudent step of ordering Geary to wait for reinforcements. Unfortunately, due to the limited road network and location of the forces involved, the help was slow in reaching the front (Sherman's four-hour delay). [71]

Setting aside the erroneous assumption made about the location of Johnston's "head of Column" (actually located near Powder Springs), Sherman made an unfair judgment of Thomas. The "splendid opportunity" was not apparent to any of the front-line commanders at the time; as has been shown, they considered themselves in a poor position. Sherman's knowledge was no greater than Thomas and Hooker; he could only have been using hindsight to criticize the actions of the Army of the Cumberland in his letter to Grant. Even if Thomas had done as Sherman desired and thrown all available forces forward immediately, they would have achieved a small victory over the Jones/Austin force, and then run into the fresh, prepared defenses of Hood's Corps at the Church. The result would have likely been the same.

This judgment of Thomas' performance was not evident in a message sent after the battle to General

McPherson, in which he described the Federal loss as "a pretty hard fight with two of Hooker's divisions." He went on to say that "To-morrow early will renew the fight if the enemy has not disappeared in the night." With Howard's Corps moving up on the Federal left and Schofield north of Howard, Sherman apparently felt that the Confederates would not risk being flanked on their right.   While tacitly acknowledging more than "twenty rebels" at New Hope Church that day, he still hoped for a quick passage through the Paulding County wilderness. It is likely that Thomas and Hooker, having borne the fury of the Confederate defense, were not so optimistic.[72]

Fighting on the Dallas Line would make an unforgettable   impression   on   many   participants. Sherman gave perhaps the best overview of the week-long struggle that began at New Hope Church: "All this time a continual battle was in progress by strong skirmish-lines, taking advantage of every species of cover, and both parties fortifying each night by rifle-trenches, with head-logs, many of which grew to be as formidable as first-class works of defense. Occasionally one party or the other would make a dash in the nature of a sally, but usually it sustained a repulse with great loss of life. I visited personally all parts of our lines nearly every day, was continually within musket-range, and though the fire of musketry and cannon resounded day and night along the whole line, . . . I rarely saw a dozen of the enemy at any one time; and these were always skirmishers dodging from tree to tree, or behind logs on the ground." [73]   The soldiers of Sherman's command felt the effects of the constant fighting as well. In one Lieutenant's words,

> We go right along about our duty in camp
> regardless of the bullets. It seems to be just
> as safe one place as another, and we have
> been subjected to this same fire most of the

day, every day for more than a month. Its our duty and we can't afford to think of it. Still, when some fellow puts a hole in your hat or coat, or a shell knocks the frying pan out of your hand and scatters your campfire in every direction, one has to stop and think a little. . . but its no use moving for you might move right in the way." [74]

The "Hell-Hole" sobriquet is most often associated with the Battle of New Hope Church, where Federal soldiers, according to General Sherman, first used the term. Historical tradition has even tied the reference to a low-lying site on the New Hope Church battlefield that has a ghost story attached! However, Sherman's original statement, taken from his memoirs, was, "This point, 'New Hope' . . .was four miles northeast of Dallas, and from the bloody fighting there *for the next week* was called by the soldiers 'Hell Hole.' " If one notices the time period (one week), it is evident Sherman meant the word "there" in this statement to refer to the fighting in the New Hope *area*, which lasted for one week. This certainly means the whole Dallas Line, not just New Hope Church.[75]

Further evidence that "Hell-Hole" refers to the Dallas Line fighting comes from the participants in those engagements. General Hazen, in his account written after the war, refers to the confusion many participants experienced when referencing Pickett's Mill and New Hope Church (see p. 45). The battle accounts of several participants in the Battle of Pickett's Mill refer to it as "New Hope", or "New Hope Church" and even as the "Hell Hole". It is apparent from this confusion over how to name a battle that many soldiers chose (just as Sherman did) the terms "New Hope" and "Hell-Hole" to label all the fighting along the Dallas Line.

The rain which began at night on May 25, would slow the campaign drastically, as well as cause further hardship to the soldiers. Sergeant Bull, in the 20th Corps, recalled twenty-one consecutive days of rain: "After one of these rains the men would be as wet as if they had fallen in a stream. As it was warm weather a wetting did not make us cold, but the ground was so saturated with water it was almost impossible to find a place in which one could rest. We would cut limbs from the bushes and lay them under our tent to keep as much as we could out of the mud, but this did not make comfortable beds." [76]

Chapter 5   **By the Left Flank**
"I cannot well work toward the left"

On the morning of May 26, realizing that the Union line extended beyond their right flank at New Hope Church, General Hood shifted Hindman's Division from his left to his right, and Cleburne's Division, (of Hardee's Corps) having been ordered the evening before to join Hood, arrived in the afternoon and was placed on Hindman's right. This extended the Confederate line to the vicinity of Pickett's Mill. Another of Hardee's divisions, Walker's, was moved to New Hope Church as additional support for Hood. These actions averted any immediate attempt the Federals might take to renew the attack at New Hope Church.

Polk's Corps had moved into position on Hood's left the night of May 25, while the remainder of Hardee's Corps, Major General Benjamin Cheatham's and Bate's Divisions, occupied positions on Polk's left, in the Dallas area. A gap existed between Bate, on the extreme left, and Cheatham's Division next to Polk. The resulting Confederate line now extended from Pickett's Mill to Dallas, eight miles long.[77]

On the morning of May 26, Hooker's Corps held roughly the same position as the night previous, at a distance of eighty to three hundred yards from the Confederate line. Geary's Division, astride the Owen's

Mill Road on Hooker's left, was initially unsupported on its left flank, but this was quickly rectified by the deployment of Howard's 4th Corps in that area. They had been the first reinforcements to arrive the night before, but had reached the battlefield after dark, too late to help out. Howard placed Brigadier General John Newton's Division on his right, joining Geary's Division at the Owen's Mill Road; then Brigadier General Thomas J. Wood's Division joined Newton. Major General David Stanley's Division was ordered to support Newton. Wood was soon able to advance his line against stiff Confederate opposition across Brown's Mill Creek to a ridge of high ground within 1/2 mile of the enemy line. On Geary's right was Butterfield's Division, with Williams' Division in reserve. [78]

Extending the Union line further to the left, the 23rd Corps moved into line joining Howard, with Hascall's Division on the right and Cox's Division on the left astride the Dallas-Acworth Road near Burnt Church (present-day Cross Roads Church). McCook's Cavalry, on Cox's left, engaged Confederate cavalry at Burnt Church late in the afternoon of the 26th, defeated them, and uncovered the enemy infantry line.[79]

The 14th Corps was dispersed between New Hope Church (Johnson's Division, supporting Howard), Burnt Hickory (Baird's Division guarding the wagons), and Dallas (Davis' Division, on the left of the 16th Corps at Dallas). This situation so frustrated the 14th Corps commander, General Palmer, that he tendered his resignation the next day. Although not accepted at this time, a later incident in August would result in Palmer's exit.[80]

On Sherman's right flank, in the vicinity of Dallas, the Army of the Tennessee prepared to advance on the town. These Federals had spent the previous night (May 25) along Pumpkinvine Creek near the Dallas-Van Wert Road bridge. Dodge's 16th Corps, camped south of the road, moved north on the morning of the 26th to take position on the left of Logan's 15th Corps at the bridge. In this alignment they moved on Dallas. By this time the main Confederate line was east of town, and only outposts remained to slow the Federal advance. These were quickly driven east beyond Dallas by Garrard's Cavalry, allowing the Army of the Tennessee's infantry an easy advance into and through the town. Opposition increased, however, as the Federals approached the main Confederate line 1-1/2 miles east of Dallas. Here Jackson's Cavalry, supported by Bate's Division of infantry, held a strong position, and forced McPherson's men to stop for reconnaissance, then deploy in line. The 15th Corps took a position southeast of Dallas, covering the Villa Rica Road; the 16th Corps formed a line east of the town, and made connection with Davis' Division (14th Corps), which had also just arrived.[81]

By the evening of May 26, the Dallas Line was completed for both sides, stretching from Dallas to Pickett's Mill. A significant gap of three miles existed in the Union line between Davis' Division, on the left of the Army of the Tennessee at Dallas and Thomas' Army of the Cumberland at New Hope Church. Attempts made by Sherman to fill this gap failed, although a line was created to join the two sections. It is likely Sherman was not concerned, however, since he was already contemplating a shift of the Army of the Tennessee toward New Hope Church.[82] As previously noted, a similar gap existed in the same area in the Confederate line.

Sherman's orders for May 27, as outlined in his "Special Field Order #12" (issued on May 26), were for a general attack on the Confederate line, beginning early in the morning. Specifically, the artillery of Hooker,

Howard, and Schofield's Corps were to begin a barrage soon after dawn, then Howard's infantry would make a right wheel (south) and capture a point of high ground commanding the New Hope Church-Marietta Road.[83] Supporting this attack, Schofield's Corps would advance on Howard's left, while Hooker's troops would "Carry some one or more points of the enemy's works to his immediate front." In a message to McPherson, Sherman explained this order as it affected the Army of the Tennessee: Davis' Division would move on the "North Marietta Road" and make a junction with Hooker at New Hope Church; Dodge would designate one division to attack on Davis' right and make connection with the left of Osterhaus' Division (15th Corps). Dodge's other division would stay in reserve while the remainder of Logan's Corps advanced along the "southerly Marietta road", running directly between Dallas and Marietta.[84]

In attempting to carry out Sherman's Special Field Order, Federal commanders encountered immediate problems. The three mile gap between Hooker and Davis was fronted by a strong line of Confederate works along Ray and Elsberry Mountains, from which an attack could be made on any attempt by Davis to shift to his left. Further, the Confederates held a very strong position on McPherson's right, in the 15th Corps sector.

At 11 am on May 27, Sherman considered the difficulty McPherson was having: "If you can't drive the enemy from his position work to your left, so as to connect with Hooker." Still later that day McPherson responded with the reason he had not made the move Sherman intended: "We have forced the enemy back to his breast-works . . . and find him occupying a strong position. . . .Our lines are up within close musket-range in many places and the enemy appear to be moving on our right. I cannot well work toward the left . . . for as soon as we uncover this flank (the right), the enemy will be on it." [85]

In the New Hope Church Sector, Thomas' attempt to execute the Order was also experiencing problems. Attempting to reconnoiter the area where Sherman intended the 4th Corps' right wheel to occur, Thomas and Howard discovered a disturbing fact: the Confederate line had been re-arranged, and extended significantly to the east.[86] (See "Dallas Line, May 27" map) Sherman's orders assumed the Confederate alignment of May 26, in which Johnston's right flank ended just northeast of New Hope Church. They probably did not realize that Cleburne's Division had also been shifted to the right; Cleburne's usual place was with Hardee's Corps, then at Dallas. Given this new situation, Thomas decided that Howard's attack on the Confederate right would have to be shifted farther to the left than anticipated.

This development, coupled with the problem encountered in the Dallas sector, forced Sherman to change his plan; instead of an attack on all fronts, Sherman would concentrate his efforts on the Confederate right. In a reply to McPherson the Federal commander's new strategy was clarified: "From [your] description I think the hills in your front are stronger than the ground to our left, by which we can move toward Allatoona and Acworth, or pound away til we find a weak place. We should have our army united." [87] Despite the problems, McPherson would be expected to connect with Hooker at New Hope Church, thereby allowing Sherman to shift his army farther to the left, around the Confederate right flank. Johnston's rapid move from Allatoona to Dallas had again denied the Federal commander access to the Confederate rear. Now, instead of looking at Marietta as the objective, Sherman was forced to shift his focus northwest to Acworth and the railroad there.

Sherman's revised plan still included Howard's attack on the left, but now embraced the tactical revision by Thomas. Instead of the 4th Corps (with the 23rd on its left) making an attack south toward the high ground along the Dallas-Acworth Rd, Howard would take a composite force, move beyond the left of the 23rd Corps, and attack the Confederate right flank. The force selected for this duty was comprised of Wood's Division, aided by Major General Richard Johnson's Division (1st) of the 14th Corps, and Brigadier General Nathaniel McLean's Brigade (1st) of the 23rd Corps, a total of 14,000 men. This decision, made without current knowledge of Confederate dispositions, profoundly affected the outcome of the battle to come.

Chapter 6 **The Battle of Pickett's Mill**
"Foredoomed to Oblivion"

U nion General William Hazen wrote:
"The Battle of Pickett's Mill was fought toward the evening of the 27th of May, 1864, and has generally been confounded with the action at New Hope Church fought two days before. . .It is scarcely noticed in any reports of the Union commanders, and is ignored by Sherman in his memoirs; but it was the most fierce, bloody, and persistent assault by our troops in the Atlanta Campaign, and the Confederates, who were victorious, have described it at length."[88]

This comment is further corroborated by fellow officers Brigadier General John King and Colonel Benjamin Scribner, who, like Hazen, commanded brigades at Pickett's Mill, yet thought the area was called New Hope Church. Another participant, in recounting his unit's action, called it "The Battle of New Hope". One soldier labeled Pickett's Mill the "Hell Hole".[89] Although ignored by General Sherman, the Battle of Pickett's Mill was considered significant by many on both sides. General Thomas Wood, commander of the Federal spearhead division in the battle, described it as "the best sustained and altogether the fiercest and most vigorous assault that was made on the enemy's entrenched positions during the entire campaign."[90] Confederate General W. W.

Mackall, Johnston's chief of staff, wrote on May 28: "In every encounter thus far we have beaten them, but have had no general engagement; last evening's was the most important and severe."[91] Therefore, despite being "confounded" with another battle, and "scarcely noticed", Pickett's Mill nevertheless made its mark on history, and at least deserves the significance given it by those who fought there.

At 10 a.m. on the 27th Stanley's Division (1st) relieved Wood's, allowing it to withdraw from the front line and form for the assault. This was accomplished in a field concealed by woods on the extreme left and rear of the 23rd Corps line. Wood's Division of 3 brigades was formed in column six lines deep, with Johnson in the rear. Thus arranged, the march began about 11 a.m. in an easterly direction.[92] These movements by the Federals to extend their line to the left did not go undetected by the Confederates. General Johnston, anticipating this move by Sherman, ordered the Confederate line extended to the right on May 26. To accomplish this, General Hood moved Hindman's Division from his left at New Hope Church to his right, and Cleburne's Division was transferred from Hardee's Corps at Dallas to the right of Hindman.[93] Arriving in the Pickett's Mill area about 2-3 p.m. on the 26th, Cleburne placed Brigadier General Lucius Polk's Brigade on Hindman's right, then Major T. R. Hotchkiss' 12-gun battalion was located on the right of Polk. Except for one regiment of Brigadier General Daniel Govan's Brigade placed to the right of Hotchkiss, the rest of the division (the brigades of Brigadier General Hiram Granbury, Govan, and Brigadier General Mark Lowrey) was placed in echelon behind Polk. The extreme right of the Confederate line now rested one mile northeast of New Hope Church. Entrenchments were erected on the front line that night and the morning of the 27th. According to Cleburne, "The

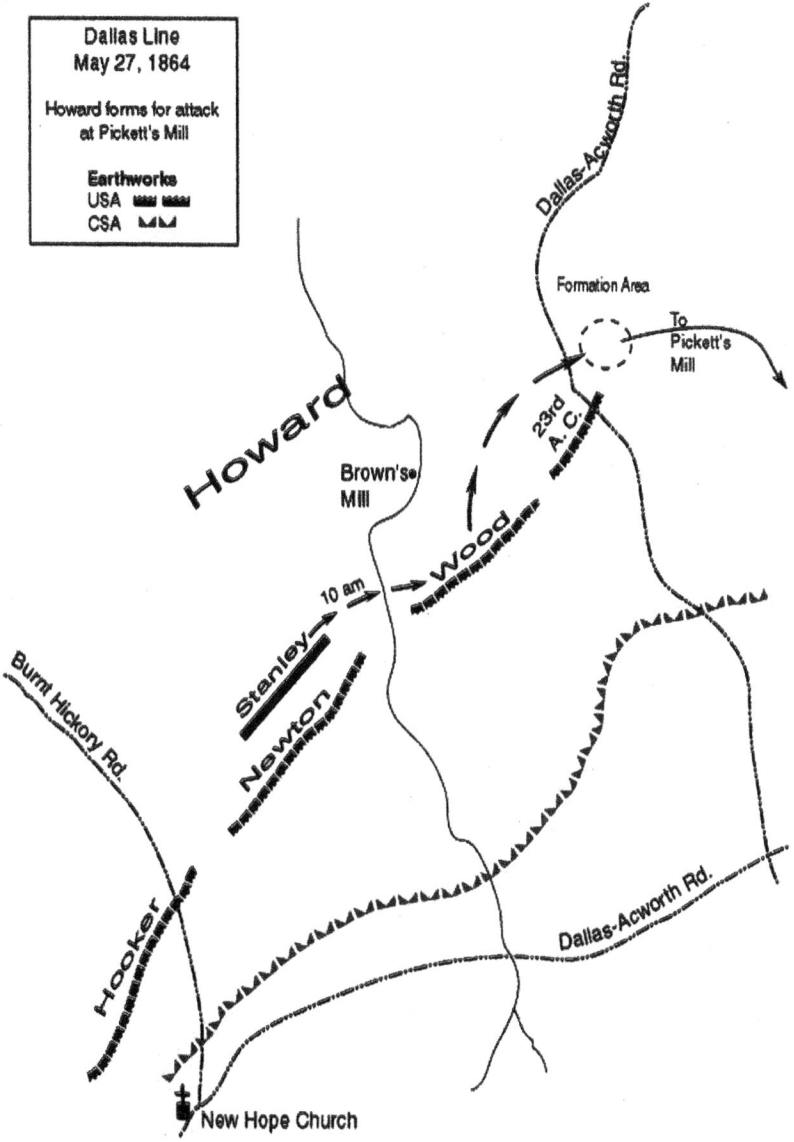

Dallas Line
May 27, 1864

Howard forms for attack
at Pickett's Mill

Earthworks
USA
CSA

position was, in the main, covered with trees and undergrowth, which served as a screen along our lines [and] concealed us, and were left standing as far as practicable for that purpose."[94] As the Federal flanking column moved eastward, many realized that the march would not be an easy one. General Wood described his men moving "through dense forests of the thickest jungle, a country whose surface was scarred by deep ravines and intersected by difficult ridges."[95] His verbal orders to Colonel Robert Kimberly, commanding the 41st Ohio (Hazen's Brigade) and leading the advance, were as follows:

> March in line of battle, skirmishers out, a mile and a half due southeast by the compass; then wheel to the right and march due southwest until the enemy [is] found. The rest of the brigade was to follow in column by battalion front, and behind were to come four other brigades. The order was explicit and emphatic to attack the instant the enemy was found, waiting for no further orders under any circumstances, whether the enemy were found in position or not, behind fortifications or otherwise.

After the wheel was accomplished, and a mile had been covered to the southwest, Kimberly saw on a wooded crest ahead: "there, in full view, 500 yards away, was a large force in position, the men busily intrenching their line. The column of attack had come upon the rear of that line, which faced the wrong way for the enemy...The attacking force was in rear of the left flank of the Union Army, instead of being in rear of the right flank of the Confederates."[96]

Howard then ordered a move by the left flank another mile eastward. This brought him to the

vicinity of Pickett's Mill about 2-3 p.m., where he and
Wood rode carefully to the front in reconnaissance.
Upon reaching the north edge of a wheat field, Howard
observed: "We still found a line of works [Govan's line]
to our right, but they did not seem to cover General
Wood's front, and they were new, the enemy still
working hard upon them." Having finally reached the
Confederate flank, the lines were readjusted for the
assault, and General Johnson's Division was brought
up on the left of Wood.[97] At 4:35pm, Howard sent a
message to Thomas outlining the situation: "I am on
the ridge beyond the hill that we were looking at this
morning. No person can appreciate the difficulty in
moving over this ground unless he can see it. I am
. . . now turning the enemy's right flank, I think."[98]

As preparations were being made, Wood
assessed the condition of his men: When all these
movements, so well calculated to try the physical
strength of the men, were concluded, and the point
gained, from which it was believed that the
column could move directly on the enemy's flank, the
day was well spent. It was nearly 4pm. The men had
been on their feet since early daylight, and of course
were much worn.[99]

The Federal plan of attack called for Wood's
Division of three brigades to attack in column of
battalions, led by Hazen's Second Brigade, followed by
the brigades of Brigadier General William Gibson (1st)
and Colonel Frederick Knefler (3rd). This formation was
designed to concentrate firepower against a small area
of the enemy line, achieve a breakthrough, and allow
further flank attacks. The same deployment, however,
had not been successful at New Hope Church, a fact
which may have affected General Howard's decision to
change the plan prior to the attack. In the presence of

General Hazen, Wood commented to Howard: "We will put in Hazen and see what success he has." Hazen later wrote: "This was a revelation to me, as it was evident there was to be no attack by column at all."[100] A member of Hazen's staff, Lieutenant Ambrose Bierce, described Hazen's reaction to this event: "For my commander and friend, my master in the art of war, . . . he uttered never a word, rode to the head of his feeble brigade and patiently awaited the command to go. Only by a look which I knew how to read did he betray his sense of the criminal blunder."[101]

The alignment of Hazen's Brigade for the assault was (as it had been throughout the march) in two lines, each containing two battalions. In the first line from left to right were the 124th, 93rd , 41st and 1st Ohio regiments. The second line was composed of (left to right) the 23rd Kentucky, 6th Indiana, 5th Kentucky, and 6th Kentucky. McLean's Brigade was assigned to protect Hazen's right flank at the edge of a wheat field. McLean was to remain "in full view of the enemy's works" to keep the Confederates in that area occupied.[102] He must have found this order confusing since he had also been commanded to maintain contact with the 23rd Corps. Due to the distance Howard had been forced to march to find the Confederate flank, the gap between Howard and the rest of the Army was about two miles. McLean had already been forced to leave skirmishers in his wake to maintain communication with Schofield's troops, and so was hard-pressed to comply with Howard's orders.

On Hazen's left flank, along Pickett's Mill Creek, the brigade of Colonel Scribner of Johnson's Division was assigned. Scribner, however, later reported he was to support the left of the next brigade behind Hazen (Gibson's)! So, in retrospect, at the very start of the advance, potential problems loomed: Hazen would have questionable support on both his flanks, and, if the

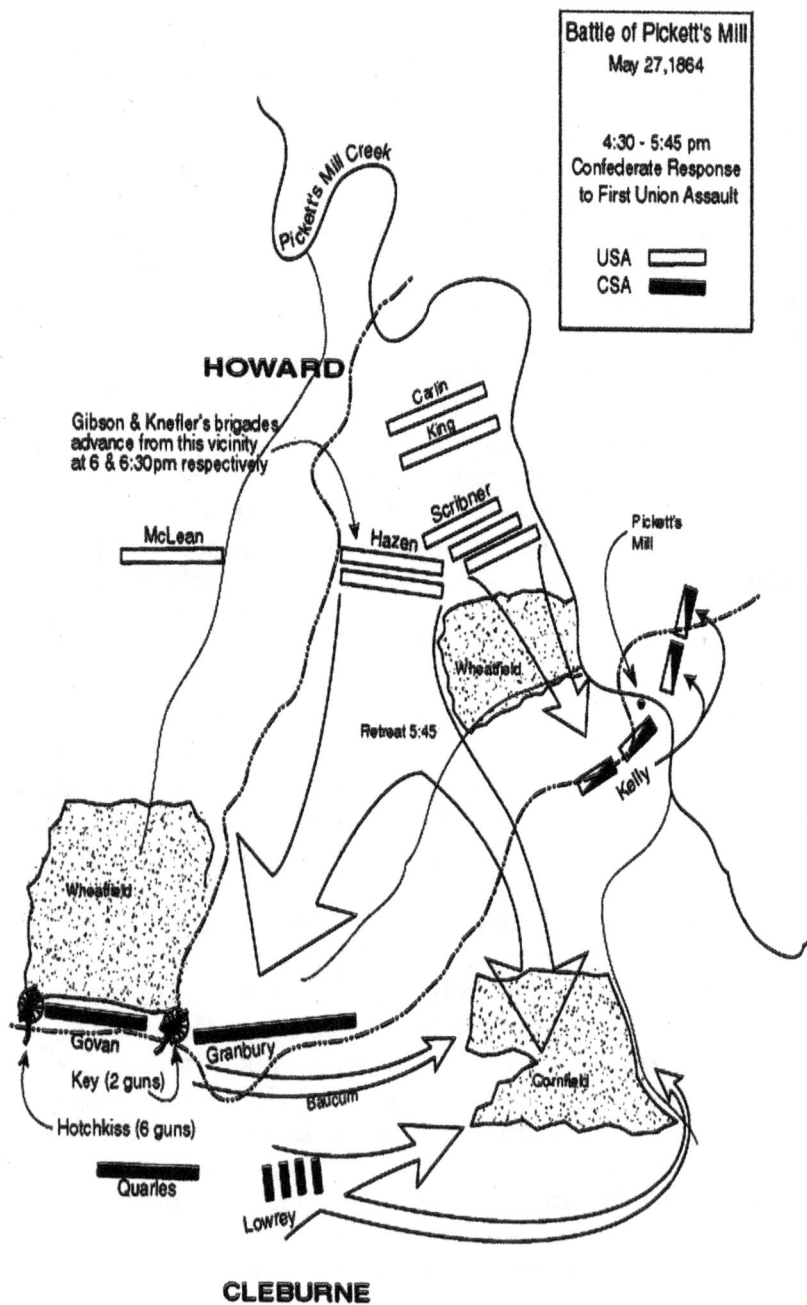

Battle of Pickett's Mill
May 27,1864

4:30 - 5:45 pm
Confederate Response
to First Union Assault

USA
CSA

Pickett's Mill Creek

HOWARD

Gibson & Knefler's brigades
advance from this vicinity
at 6 & 6:30pm respectively

Carlin

King

Scribner

McLean   Hazen

Pickett's
Mill

Wheatfield

Retreat 5:45

Kelly

Wheatfield

Cornfield

Govan   Granbury

Key (2 guns)   Baucum

Hotchkiss (6 guns)

Quarles

Lowrey

CLEBURNE

column attack was not properly supported, he would lack support behind him as well. According to Bierce: "That, then, was the situation: a weak brigade of fifteen hundred men, with masses of idle troops behind in the character of audience, waiting for the word to march a quarter-mile uphill."[103]   At 4:30 p.m. on May 27th, General Wood gave the order to advance, and Hazen moved forward, unsupported, and unaware of what lay before him.[104]

Throughout the Federal march to Pickett's Mill, General Cleburne had been busy establishing his defense for the expected attack. General Govan's Brigade was sent on the morning of May 27 toward the Federal line with orders to report any movements by   the enemy. About 11am, close to the time the Federal march began, Cleburne had received word from Govan that the enemy was moving to the right.   Govan was then ordered back to the line and placed on the right of Polk's Brigade "where he covered himself in rifle pits." To bolster the defense further, Cleburne placed on Govan's right two 12-pounder howitzers from Hotchkiss' battalion under the command of Captain Thomas J. Key. These guns were sighted to enfilade a deep ravine near his front. It was in this area that Cleburne expected the main Federal attack to occur.[105]

About 4pm, as the Federal column was forming for the assault, Cleburne ordered Hiram Granbury's Texas Brigade to form on the right of Govan. Lieutenant R. M. Collins, of the 15th Texas, described the scene: "A courier dashed up to Granbury's headquarters under a great oak, and handed him a dispatch. The General did not wait to send orders to the commanders of regiments to get their regiments ready to move but rose up at once and gave the command: 'Attention Brigade!'. We were in line, every man in his place, in less time than it requires to pencil four of these lines, at the command 'Right face,

forward, double quick march!' we were off on a run."
Granbury's men thus quickly moved to the right the
length of their brigade, formed line of battle, and moved
a short distance downhill to receive the Federal
attack.[106]

The position they now occupied was along a spur
ridge running northeast from a point near the junction
of Govan's right and Granbury's left. Between this spur
and another ridge running north from the Confederate
line opposite Granbury's left "was a deep ravine, the
side of which next to Granbury was very steep, with
occasional benches of rock, up to a line within 30 or 40
yards of Granbury's men, where it flattened into a
natural glacis. This glacis was well covered with well
grown trees, and in most places with thick
undergrowth."[107] Such terrain, with the addition of
fieldworks (not entrenchments), made Granbury's line
much easier to defend, as was soon proven. The
remainder of the Confederate line, from the right flank
of Granbury to Pickett's Mill Creek, was held by
Brigadier General John Kelly's cavalry Division (of
Wheeler's Corps) with about 1000 men, dismounted.[108]

Against this line Hazen's men were now moving,
and were soon in the midst of the thick undergrowth
described by Cleburne. Bierce   provides   the   best
account   of   the struggle:

> We moved forward. In less than one minute
> the   trim battalions had become simply a
> swarm   of   men   struggling   through   the
> undergrowth   of   the   forest,   pushing   and
> crowding. The front was irregularly serrated,
> the strongest and bravest in advance, the
> others   following in   fan-like   formations,
> variable   and   inconstant,   ever   defining
> themselves anew. . .The color bearers kept
> well   to   the   front   with their flags, closely
> furled, aslant backward over their shoulders.

Displayed, they would have been torn to rags by the boughs of the trees. Horses were all sent to the rear; the general [Hazen] and staff and all the field officers toiled along on foot as best they could.

As the men moved on, closer and closer to the Confederate line,

Suddenly there were [sic] a ringing rattle of musketry, the familiar hissing of bullets, and before us the interspaces of the forest were all blue with smoke. Hoarse, fierce yells broke out of a thousand throats. The forward fringe of brave and hardy assailants was arrested in its mutable extensions; the edge of our swarm grew dense and clearly defined as the foremost halted, and the rest pressed forward to align themselves beside them, all firing. The uproar was deafening; the air was sibilant with streams and sheets of missiles. In the steady, unvarying roar of small-arms the frequent shock of the cannon was rather felt than heard, but the gusts of grape which they blew into that populous wood were audible enough, screaming among the trees and cracking against their stems and branches. We had, of course, no artillery to reply.[109]

This intense fire from Granbury's men began to take its toll on the right of Hazen's line. According to Cleburne, as the Federals charged they shouted "'Ah, damn you, we have caught you without your logs now.' [a reference to New Hope Church]. Granbury's men, needing no logs, were awaiting them, and throughout awaited them with calm determination, and as they appeared on the slope slaughtered them with deliberate aim. The piles of his dead on this front, pronounced by the officers of this army who have seen most service to be greater than they had ever seen before, were a silent but sufficient eulogy upon Granbury and his noble Texans."[110]

Such was the situation on the Federal right, in the ravine, subjected as it was to the canister from Key's howitzers and musketry from Granbury, at a range of less than 100 yards. On the Federal left, however, conditions were considerably different. In the confusion of the advance, Hazen's supporting line of two battalions had, "on account of the thick wood", lost contact with the first line, and changed direction to the left. Whether by accident or intention, this move brought the second line to the vicinity of the cornfield, where it joined the left flank of the first line, already engaged with Granbury.[111] In effect then, what began as a column assault ended with Hazen's Brigade stretched out in line of battle. Instead of being overlapped by Granbury, as they would have been had they continued in their initial formation, Hazen's second line now extended beyond the Confederate flank, and reached the cornfield some 40 to 50 yards in the enemy rear. As these men advanced across the cornfield, the 23rd Kentucky on the left adjacent to a stream, the 6th Indiana in the center, and the 5th and 6th Kentucky on the right, the door to the Confederate rear lay open, with "no works and but slight resistance in [their] front."[112]

General Granbury, however, was aware of the disaster about to occur, and quickly sent a message to General Govan on his left, asking for help to extend the line. At this time Govan was not opposed by any significant number of the enemy, contrary to the intent of General Howard. Instead of acting to "attract the enemy's attention and draw his fire" as ordered, McLean had allowed his brigade to remain hidden in the woods at the edge of the wheat field.[113]

Govan was therefore able to respond quickly to Granbury's call for assistance. Colonel G. F. Baucum's consolidated 8th and 19th Arkansas was "hastily" withdrawn from the line and sent to the extreme Confederate right. Here they confronted Hazen's Brigade, which had just overrun the fieldworks held by Kelly's dismounted cavalry. Baucum made a "sweeping charge", but failed to stop the Federal advance, being himself flanked instead. Aware of the crisis developing on his right, Cleburne moved his last brigade, Lowrey's, to the threatened area. "His arrival was most opportune," Cleburne said, "as the enemy was beginning to pour around Baucum's right." As Lowrey arrived, "throwing his regiments in successively as they unmasked themselves by their flank march," the Federals began to realize that "slight resistance" was quickly becoming otherwise.[114] In an excellent account of the cornfield fight, C. C. Briant of the 6th Indiana described the situation at this time on the Federal side. As the 23rd Kentucky and 6th Indiana reached the south side of the cornfield, the discovery was made that the 5th Kentucky, on the right of the 6th, had stopped a short distance back in some woods projecting from the southwest corner of the field. Briant was sent to bring up these troops to protect the right of the Federal line. After delivering his message to Colonel Berry of the 5th, Briant returned to his regiment only to find that Captain Samuel McKeehan, then the ranking officer in that area, had been shot in the mouth and lay on the ground. Briant continues:

> I laid his [McKeehan's] head back on the ground and straightened up with my face full to the front. The first look discovered a rebel column in good order [Lowrey] moving at quick time toward Pumpkin Vine Creek. I thought this meant mischief, and broke at the top of my speed to the left, down the line

toward the creek, passing to the bluff beyond
the extreme left   of the   Twenty-third
Kentucky. From here I could see no help
anywhere; but this rebel column had passed
by our left, down the creek, and were just
coming into the   field at the mouth of the
ravine   [in   the   cornfield],   and in five
minutes   more   time   would   have been
completely in our rear. I instantly gave the
command to retreat, and at the same time,
with all possible speed, went back up to my
own regiment, yelling at the top of my voice
all the way up, `Retreat! Retreat!' and as soon
as I arrived at my own regiment and company
I gave the order, `Retreat square to the rear or
we will be captured.' It is needless to say that
both regiments broke in wild disorder for a
place of safety. But the amusing part of this
performance was to see the rebel commander
ride in   the   midst of   the   Twenty-third
Kentucky boys, and with a   very   gentle,
sweet voice, tell them to halt and form their
lines, while his own men, with fixed bayonets,
were coming as fast as   their legs   would
carry them. The boys did not halt, all the
same.   But the curious part was that they
were so   much   excited that they did not
notice the rebel Colonel, but made their way
into our own line and were saved, except a
few on the extreme left, near the creek.[115]

    Although forced to retreat across the cornfield in
"wild disorder", the Federals reformed along the fence
at its north edge. General Hazen recounted this event:
"The left flank fell back along the fence near my
position [the fence] running at right angles to the
line of battle . . . and here fired with great execution
upon the enemy advancing across the cornfield from

our   left. The enemy came on in fine style, coming up from the ravine beyond; but after one volley from our men along the fence they were out of sight, to a man, in twenty seconds."[116]

Cleburne   states   that   the   advancing Confederates, "finding themselves suffering from the enemy's direct and oblique fire, withdrew, passing over the open space of the field behind them." This withdrawal, however, was mistaken for a repulse by some of Cleburne's staff, who falsely assumed the Confederate line had been broken.   They quickly brought up William A. Quarles' Brigade (from Stewart's Division)   to restore the line, but finding it intact, repositioned Quarles behind Lowrey as a reserve. The Confederate line then occupied a position extending along the south edge of the cornfield and across a creek east to a hill.[117]

This action on the Federal left was the closest Howard's men   would come to victory at Pickett's Mill, and ironically, was the   result of an unplanned change in formation.   Only by an alert Confederate response was the Federal assault on Granbury's flank repulsed, and disaster averted. In the words of General Lowrey, "the position [of Granbury] could not have been held had not the right flank been secured. . .Indeed it was one of those times in which the victory trembled in the scale, and the lives of many men, and probably the destiny of an army, hung upon   a moment of time."[118] The scale may indeed have been tipped in   favor of the Federals had Scribner's Brigade   arrived to support Hazen. This was prevented by the action of General John H. Kelly's cavalry in the vicinity of Pickett's Mill.[119]

Anticipating a Federal advance along the stream, Kelly had deployed his men dismounted along a hill southwest of the Mill. When Colonel Scribner's Federal Brigade advanced (shortly after Hazen) with its left flank along the creek, some of Kelly's men crossed the creek at the Mill and poured a deadly enfilading fire into Scribner's men. Scribner, unaware that Hazen was desperately in need of support, stopped his advance to take action against the Confederates on his left. He put three regiments across the creek just north of the Mill and assaulted the hill opposite it. The Confederates were driven off the hill, but not before critical time had been lost. Hazen was then fighting in the cornfield, where Scribner's absence was sorely felt.[120]

Hazen's regiments were just about to their limit of endurance. Pressured on the left by Lowrey's and Quarles' brigades, and decimated on the right in the ravine, Hazen sent back messages for help. Many of the couriers carrying these messages were shot as they moved to the rear, however, while others, finding their way back, failed to find the expected support.[121] This news, coupled with the increased pressure on both his flanks, caused Hazen to order a withdrawal. Many units were unable to retreat due to heavy Confederate fire, however, and remained on the line. Those that could withdraw began to fall back all along the line, from ravine to cornfield. In Bierce's words,

> The battle, as a battle, was at an end, but there was still some slaughter that it was possible to incur before nightfall; and as the wreck of our brigade drifted back through the forest we met the brigade (Gibson's) which, had the attack been made in column, as it should have been, would have been but five minutes behind our heels, with another [brigade] five minutes behind its own. As it was, just forty-five minutes had elapsed, during which the enemy had destroyed us and was now ready to perform the same kindly office to our successors.[122]

Several fragments of regiments that had assembled in the rear after the Federal withdrawal passed by Howard and Hazen. As recorded by Pvt. Silas Crowell (93rd Ohio), a lieutenant leading this group stepped up to Hazen and said, "General, where is our brigade?. . .We wish to report our regiments. General Hazen looked at him a moment. The tears began to roll down his cheeks and he said, `Brigade, hell, I have none. But what is left is over there in the woods.'"[123]

General Hazen later gave his brigade high praise for their effort at Pickett's Mill: "It is due the brave brigade. . .to say that this battle of the 27th of May is its first and only unsuccessful effort during the war, and at this time, as its dead list will show, went at its work with an honest good will which deserved a better result. I shall ever believe its part bravely and well done."[124]

It is at this point in the battle that the failure to carry out the original plan of action begins to have its effect. As Bierce pointed out, Gibson's Brigade was not in immediate supporting distance as Hazen advanced. That General Wood had to order Gibson to "renew the assault" indicates that the plan for a column of brigades assault had never been followed through, or had not been made sufficiently clear to the commanders.[125] Several of Hazen's regimental commanders, in their after-action reports, said that had a "second line" been available, they could have carried the portion of the enemy line to their front. Why the supporting brigades of Wood's Division were not close at hand is unclear, the most likely reason being the difficult terrain and poor visibility. Under these conditions neither Wood nor Howard was able to see enough to realize Hazen's situation. In any event, as Bierce noted, Gibson's help came too late.

General Wood had hoped that a renewed assault by Gibson would prove successful for several reasons: Gibson would have a shorter distance to advance than had Hazen; he would have knowledge of the ground gained by Hazen; and perhaps by this time Scribner had provided cover for the left flank.[126] However, in the interval between the withdrawal of Hazen and the launching of an assault by Gibson, the Confederates had strengthened their line with fieldworks, re-supplied their ammunition, and received reinforcements. Scribner was still to the rear, engaged with Kelly's cavalry; thus, despite Wood's hopes, Gibson was to suffer a worse fate than Hazen.

As he moved forward about 6pm, Gibson encountered the thick woods that had so impaired Hazen. One of his men wrote that "The woods and undergrowth were so dense that nothing could be seen for a distance of one-hundred fifty yards." As a result, the two advancing lines of Gibson's Brigade lost contact with each other, and the first line drifted to the left. Lieutenant Colonel Samuel F. Gray, of the 49th Ohio (now on the front line) described his approach to the Confederate position: "I could see no organized force in my front, but the woods full of men seeking shelter from the terrible storm of shot and shell." At this point Gray met the Adjutant General of Hazen's Brigade, who told him that the Confederate line was across a ravine "a few yards in advance." When the 49th Ohio arrived at the ravine, they could see remnants of Hazen's Brigade below the crest of the hill on the other side, with the Confederate line beyond. As Gibson's Federals charged up the hill they were enfiladed by artillery and musketry from the right, and a storm of fire in front. Despite this, they pressed on, advancing to within 10 paces of the enemy line, and in some places "occupying one side of his barricade and he the other." However, according to Gray, "it was found impossible for us to take a position before which line after line had melted away. . ."[127]   Thus, to retain their position, Gibson's men began to seek cover on the side of the hill, hoping for reinforcements. They, as Hazen did before them, waited in vain. Gibson soon found himself enveloped on both flanks, and hard pressed in front, which forced him to the same conclusion as Hazen: retreat.   When the order was given, many units began to fall back to the shelter of the ravine, and then to the rear. Here again, however, some units could not risk a withdrawal without exposing   themselves to heavy enemy fire, so they joined Hazen's men clinging to the cover afforded them by the trees and rocks along the hillside closest to the Confederate line.   From these positions the intermingled men of Gibson's and Hazen's brigades maintained an   incessant fire on the enemy. Later reports would show the heavier beating Gibson had suffered: his loss totaled 681, while that of Hazen was 467. Sgt. Andrew Gleason of the 15th Ohio spoke for many of the survivors: "This is surely not war, it is butchery."[128]

At this point, as darkness approached (about 7pm), Wood and Howard decided that further assaults were useless. This was most likely a direct result of a message received from General Thomas. As recorded in the IV Corps journal at 6pm, this dispatch ordered Howard to: "connect his right with General Schofield's left, and to take up a strong position which he could hold until he can be re-enforced, and if necessary to do this our left must be refused; that he must not place his troops in such a position as to risk being turned, and to say to General Johnson that he must place his troops so as to secure our left flank."[129] There were, however, large numbers of Federal dead and wounded remaining in the ravine and along the hillside before the Confederate line. To rescue these men, Wood ordered his last brigade, under Colonel Knefler, to move forward.   He was not to make an assault, but to maintain the Federal line long enough to recover the wounded. Thus, two hours late, the third Federal brigade made its advance through the ravine, and, as their comrades before them, found it impossible to maintain their formation. As Knefler's men reached the Confederate line, they, too were "completely enfiladed by the enemy's artillery, suffering severely."[130] Subjected to such intense fire, the Federals were forced to fight desperately to cling to their position, and resorted to building barricades close to the Confederate line.

Meanwhile, at Pickett's Mill, Colonel Scribner's men had driven the Confederate cavalry off the hill on the east side of the creek and were advancing south astride the stream.   They were probably unaware of Hazen's and Gibson's defeats, until they arrived at the cornfield to join the left flank of Knefler (the 17th Ky.). Thus, finally, the Federal line was established on   the left of Wood, although too late to achieve victory. Instead of arriving on an open Confederate flank as they might have earlier, Scribner's men found the brigades of Lowrey and Quarles behind fieldworks at the south edge of the cornfield. According to Scribner, "The enemy, emboldened by his success in checking our progress, furiously assaulted the whole line; this was   repeated several times and as often repulsed.[131] When it was finally dark the combat lulled, and each side kept up a sporadic fire on the other. The goal of Knefler's advance, retrieval of the wounded, was not yet accomplished, and would not be. Knefler later recounted that many of the wounded were left on the field due to "the impossibility of bringing ambulances to the scene of action, it being an almost impenetrable jungle, cut up by ravines, creeks, and swamps, without roads, or even paths, for vehicles of any description."[132]

Troops on both sides took what rest was possible at such close quarters; barely 100 yards separated them, and in some places less. General Cleburne described this situation: "For some hours afterwards [after dark] a desultory dropping fire, with short, vehement bursts of musketry, continued, the enemy lying in great numbers immediately in front of portions of my line, and so near it that their footsteps could be distinctly heard."[133]

Unable to rest his men under these conditions, General Granbury obtained permission from Cleburne to make an assault on the enemy to his front. This was primarily Knefler's Brigade, but also included the remnants of Hazen's and Gibson's units. Around 10pm Granbury's men moved forward, their places in line being immediately occupied by Brigadier General Edward C. Walthall's brigade of Hindman's Division. According to Collins, "at the sound of the bugle we dashed down, with a yell, into that dark gorge, like a whirlwind."[134] Cleburne adds his description: "The Texans, their bayonets fixed, plunged into the darkness...and with one bound were upon the enemy; but they met with no resistance. Surprised and panic-stricken, many fled, escaping in the darkness; others surrendered and were brought into our lines."[135]

From the Federal perspective, however, this night attack takes on a different character. Wood recounted that Knefler's men fired a volley into the advancing Confederates, which brought them to a "dead halt", after which Knefler was "handsomely and skillfully withdrawn", and "not the slightest pursuit was attempted."[136] A just rendering of the accounts gives the impression that the Confederates charged, some Federals fled, while most of them held their line for a quick volley and then withdrew hastily, if not in panic. One last Confederate account comes from Captain Samuel T. Foster, and serves to give a balanced view:

"In about an hour from the time we rec'd Granburys order to charge . . .we raised a regular Texas yell. . .and started forward through the brush, and so dark we could not see anything at all. We commenced to fire as soon as we started, and the Yanks turned loose, and the flash of their guns would light up the woods like a flash of lightning, and by it we could see a line of blue coats just there in front of us."[137]

The retreat of Knefler on the right of the Federal line posed a serious problem for Scribner on the left. With his right flank exposed, he was vulnerable to attack, should Granbury take advantage of the opportunity. Scribner wisely ordered the 74th Ohio, his reserve, to occupy with a skirmish line the left of Knefler's vacated position. When Confederate skirmishers on Granbury's right met this line, "they were not aware of any material change in our [Scribner's] lines."[138] Later, around midnight, Scribner was withdrawn to a position in the rear, and the field of conflict was left in Confederate hands. As the Federal brigades retreated from the front, they were placed about one-half mile to the rear along a line of breastworks begun during the battle. These works, started on the left by Carlin and King's brigades of Johnson's Division, were most likely the result of Thomas' telegram to Howard. The line thus formed was held from left to right by Carlin's Brigade (placed east of Pickett's Mill Creek later that evening), then King with Scribner in reserve, and finally the remnants of Hazen, Gibson, and Knefler's brigades on the right. Carlin and King were ready should the Confederates attempt a counterattack the next day. Everyone dug in, occasionally glancing in the direction of the Battlefield, where dead pine trees had caught fire and, in one soldier's words," cast a weired [sic] and gloomy light."[139]

On the following day, May 28th, neither side was able to renew the fight. Instead, Confederates and Federals began regrouping, fortifying, and surveying the carnage before them. One Union soldier remarked: "I was over the battleground. . .and never even at Shiloh, have I seen trees on the ground, marked as these. In one tree we counted two hundred bullet marks."[140] There was also a large number of Federal dead lying close to the Confederate line. Lieutenant R. M. Collins, of Granbury's Brigade, wrote that daylight on May 28 at Pickett's Mill "revealed a sight on that hill side that was sickening to look upon. All along in front of the center and left of our brigade the ground was literally covered with dead men. To look upon this and then the beautiful wild woods, the pretty flowers as they drank in the morning dew, and listen to the sweet notes of the songsters in God's first temples, we were constrained to say, 'What is man and his destiny, to do such a strange thing?' "[141]

Perhaps the most gruesome account of the aftermath at Pickett's Mill comes from the diary of Captain Foster:

May 28th

About sun up this morning we were relieved and ordered back to the Brigade--and we have to pass over the dead Yanks of the battle field of yesterday; and here I beheld that which I cannot describe; and which I hope never to see again, dead men meet the eye in every direction, and in one place I stoped [sic] and counted 50 dead men in a circle of 30 ft. of me. Men lying in all sorts of shapes and [illegible] just as they had fallen, and it seems like they have nearly all been shot in the head, and a great number of them have their skulls bursted open and their brains

running out, quite a number that way. I have
seen many dead men, and seen them
wounded and crippled in various ways, have
seen their limbs cut off, but I never saw
anything before that made me sick, like
looking at the brains of these men did. I do
believe that if a soldier could be made to faint,
that I would have fainted if I had not passed
on and got out of that place as soon as I did--
We learn thru [sic] Col Wilkes that we killed
703 dead on the ground, and captured near
350 prisoners.[142]

These Federal dead, totaling from 500-700
according to various accounts, were buried along the
Confederate line.[143] Despite this, one Federal soldier
remarked, "The stench from dead horses and dead men
between the lines was almost intolerable. No wonder
the boys named it 'Hell Hole'."[144]

Cleburne, who's loss at Pickett's Mill was 85
killed and 363 wounded, surveyed the Federal dead
and estimated the enemy loss at not less than 3000
killed and wounded.[145] This figure was based on the
usual ratio of dead to wounded, one to four. This ratio,
however, was not applicable at Pickett's Mill, as
indicated by Bierce: "I remember that we were all
astonished at the uncommonly large proportion of dead
to wounded--a consequence of the uncommonly close
range at which most of the fighting was done."[146] The
ratio of dead to wounded for Wood's Division (losses for
Scribner's Brigade were not found) was actually 1 to
2.5, higher than any battle in the Atlanta Campaign, as
well as most other Civil War battles. Total Federal
losses were about 1600.[147] Generals Howard and
Johnson both suffered wounds during the fight.
Howard was hit during the battle by a shell fragment,
which bruised his foot, and forced him to sit that night
among the other wounded. Johnson received his injury

on the night after the battle while he was sleeping--"a cannon-ball came bounding along the ground and stuck [him] in the side." The wound was serious enough to force Johnson to relinquish his command for a short time.[148]

The heavy Federal losses at Pickett's Mill not only indicate the close range at which the battle was fought, but also the determination that the Federals displayed while attacking. While the Confederates were no less determined, the effort evidenced by Howard's men in such a pernicious situation is worthy of high praise. As Hazen said, his men "deserved a better result." Hazen's was the most out-spoken criticism directed against Howard after the battle. Hazen and Ambrose Bierce were vehement in their complaints that the initial plan of attack, a massed assault in column of brigades, was abandoned just prior to the start of the battle. Instead of a concentrated assault on a narrow front, Howard sent in his brigades individually, at intervals, allowing the Confederates breathing room between attacks. Several other Federal officers in the attack later reported that if support had been available, they could have broken the enemy line. A second criticism of Howard concerned his handling of the Federal left flank, along Pickett's Mill Creek. Brigadier General Jacob D. Cox, commanding a Division of the 23rd Federal Corps at the time, made the following comment after the War: "Had Johnson [Scribner's division commander] noticed that he was first attacked in flank by cavalry only, and pushed Scribner's Brigade straight on in support of Hazen, whilst he took care of the horsemen with another brigade of his division, the determined attack of the Fourth Corps men would probably have been successful."[149]

Howard himself chastises General McLean for failure to make a "demonstration" against the Confederate left. It was this failure, he says, that allowed the enemy to reinforce their right by withdrawing Baucum's troops from their left.

The foregoing criticisms, however, must be weighed in light   of the situation as Howard experienced it, rather than in hindsight. Several considerations are helpful in this regard. First, and most important, the Federal march to Pickett's Mill extended the Union line beyond the point of continuity. When Thomas and Howard changed the initial point of attack on the morning of the 27th, they did not realize that the Confederates had extended their right flank by shifting Hindman's and Cleburne's divisions to the right. This move forced Howard's flanking force to make a much more lengthy march to their left   than was originally anticipated. McLean's Brigade, in addition to making a demonstration on the right, was also assigned the role of maintaining contact with the left flank of the Federal Army at New Hope Church. When the Battle commenced, McLean had only a thin line of skirmishers to maintain contact with the 23rd Corps to his right, leaving the 14,000 men at Pickett's Mill effectively isolated, with no road for supply or reinforcement. On the other hand, the roads from the New Hope Church area to Cleburne's position at Pickett's Mill provided an easy reinforcement route for the Confederates. This route was utilized during the battle by two brigades (Quarles and Walthall) sent to reinforce Cleburne, increasing his available force from 5700 at the beginning of the fight to approximately 10,000 (including cavalry) at the end.[150] The relative ease with which the Confederates were able to reinforce their position, coupled with Howard's separation from the Federal army, probably brought him to the obvious deduction: his men were ripe for a counterattack should they fail at Pickett's Mill. If one is to second-guess Howard, these facts are essential for a fair appraisal. Howard's decision not to pursue the column attack, as well as his apparent reluctance to support his left flank, can in part be justified by the fact of his isolation from the rest of the Federal Army. Undoubtedly he was aware of this situation when he arrived at Pickett's Mill, and at the same time he was unaware of the strength of his enemy. If this was indeed the case, sending Hazen in as a forced reconnaissance was a reasonable decision; likewise his decision (if there was one) not to support Scribner on the left. At that point his last fresh troops, the brigades of King and Carlin, were in position. There was no hope of reinforcement or re-supply that day. Without artillery, and realizing he faced an aggressive enemy with ample reinforcements, holding these units in reserve was a prudent choice. Even had he failed to ascertain this predicament, Thomas' message at 6pm would have had the same effect. Indeed, the entrenching begun by   King's Brigade while in reserve may have been a direct result of   this dispatch. Another consideration on Howard's behalf was the terrain disadvantages with which he had to contend. According to Cox: "The ground. . .was a dense wood broken into ravines, where nothing could be seen, and where the embarrassments were scarcely less than in a night attack. Under the circumstances the wonder is, not that the attack failed, it is rather that Howard was able to withdraw in order, carrying off his wounded; and that he did so proves the magnificent steadiness and courage of his officers and men."[151]

An adequate reconnaissance was essential in such a situation, but the time it had taken to find the Confederate flank, coupled with the need to attack before the enemy could erect earthworks, meant little time for reconnaissance. Pressed with the need to efficiently coordinate and maneuver troops through the dense woods, Howard lacked the information necessary to successfully prosecute the battle. Normally, information was supplied to a commander by messengers, or line of sight, but at Pickett's Mill line of sight was severely limited, and messengers often got lost or killed. Howard, as a result, was effectively blind as a commander in the battle.

The Federal and Confederate troops remained in position for several days after the Battle. Each side entrenched, the Confederates along the Pickett's Mill road, the Federals one-half mile north. During the night of the 27th a road was constructed from the Federal rear to the nearest existing road, allowing ammunition, as well as artillery, to be brought up in support of the weary infantry. Also that night Carlin's Brigade of Johnson's Division was placed across Pickett's Mill Creek, on the left of King's Brigade.[152] This action was in compliance with General Thomas' message to Howard. By the 28th, the Federals had been re-supplied, and communication with the rest of the Federal Army had been re-established.[153] The artillery was entrenched as well, and engaged in counter-battery fire with Confederate cannon.

The Battle of Pickett's Mill is not mentioned in Sherman's Memoirs. The only reference is to Howard's wound: "I hope Howard is not seriously injured, enough to lose his services."[154] Perhaps the Federal commander was too embarrassed by the failure, but it seems just as likely that he did not consider it significant. It was thus "foredoomed to oblivion".

Chapter 7   **Action in the Dallas Sector**
"A Continual Battle"

At this point in the action, Sherman's perception of the campaign is reflected in a telegram to Halleck, dated May 28, 6 a.m.:

> The enemy discovered my move to turn Allatoona, and moved to meet us there. . . . Here [New Hope Church] Johnston has chosen a strong line, . . . and has thus far stopped us. My right is Dallas, center about 3 miles north, and I am gradually working around by the left to approach the railroad anywhere in front of Acworth. Country very densely wooded and broken. No roads of any consequence. We have had many sharp, severe encounters, but nothing decisive. Both sides duly cautious in the obscurity of the ambushed ground. [155]

Sherman thus re-confirmed the main objective in his move toward Dallas (forcing the Confederates out of the Allatoona Mountains), and also admits that his hopes of gaining further advantages (cutting the Confederate supply line at Marietta) are gone. Perhaps alluding to his losses at New Hope Church and Pickett's Mill, Sherman recorded in his Memoirs:

> All this time a continual battle was in progress by strong skirmish-lines, taking advantage of

every species of cover, and both parties
fortifying each night. . . . Occasionally one
party or the other would make a dash in the
nature of a sally, but usually it sustained a
repulse with great loss of life. . . .I rarely saw a
dozen of the enemy at any one time; and these
were always skirmishers dodging from tree to
tree, or behind logs on the ground, or who
occasionally showed their heads above the
hastily-constructed but remarkably strong
rifle-trenches. [156]

From this account, Sherman's frustration with the
progress made thus far is readily apparent.
Nevertheless, he persisted with his goal of shifting the
Federal Army to the left.

On May 27, while Howard struggled at Pickett's
Mill, Edward McCook's Federal Cavalry maintained a
tenuous hold on a critical road junction opposite the
Confederate right flank. In a line facing southeast
along the "Marietta road" (present-day Due West Road)
on the extreme left of the Federal Army, McCook
warned Sherman that if the Federal cavalry were driven
away, the Confederates would have access to "the rear
of our whole infantry line." [157]   Despite McCook's
concern, however, no reinforcements arrived to support
him. Johnston's attention remained focused on other
parts of his line, and McCook was not seriously
threatened. This area would soon play an important
role in Sherman's east-ward shift.

That same day between New Hope Church and
Dallas, an attempt was made to fill the gap existing on
Hooker's right flank. Jefferson C. Davis, whose division
held the left of the Federal forces around Dallas, sent
Colonel Dan McCook's (3rd) Brigade toward a pass
between Ray and Elsberry Mountains. In addition to
decreasing the gap, this action protected the Federal
center from any Confederate attack via this mountain

pass, and threatened the same from the Federal side. Colonel John Mitchell's (2nd) Brigade also contributed one regiment, the 34th Illinois, which established a picket line between Davis and Hooker.[158]   Although the Confederates made repeated skirmish attacks in this area, (all repulsed), it is unlikely that Johnston was aware of the gap in the Federal center. The resistance encountered in their attacks, as well as the difficult terrain, kept the Confederates ignorant of this Federal weakness.

On Davis' right, McPherson still labored to extricate his army from close contact with the Confederates. The Federal line was well-fortified by this time, but still embroiled in heavy skirmishing with Hardee's Corps.   The 16th Corps was deployed (facing southeast) with Brigadier General James C. Veatch's (4th) Division on the left, connecting with Davis' Division, and Brigadier General Thomas W. Sweeny's (2nd) Division on the right, connecting with the left of Osterhaus' Division, 15th Corps.   To the right of Osterhaus, the remaining divisions of the 15th Corps were arrayed: Smith's (2nd), followed by Harrow's (4th) astride the south Villa Rica road.[159]   Captain Francis DeGress' Battery, the 1st Illinois Light (composed of four 20-pound Parrott rifles) occupied a place in the line of Harrow's Division.   They were located here primarily to "engage a rebel battery of eight guns 1,200 yards off".   This Confederate battery was actually the two batteries of Captain Frank Gracey (Cobb's Kentucky) and Captain Cuthbert Slocomb (Washington Light Artillery or Louisiana Battery).[160]   The extreme right of the 15th Corps line was held by Colonel John Wilder's "Lightning Brigade", so named for their large number of Spencer repeating rifles. They were posted on a hill to the right of Harrow's Division, and would play a major role in the fighting to come.[161]

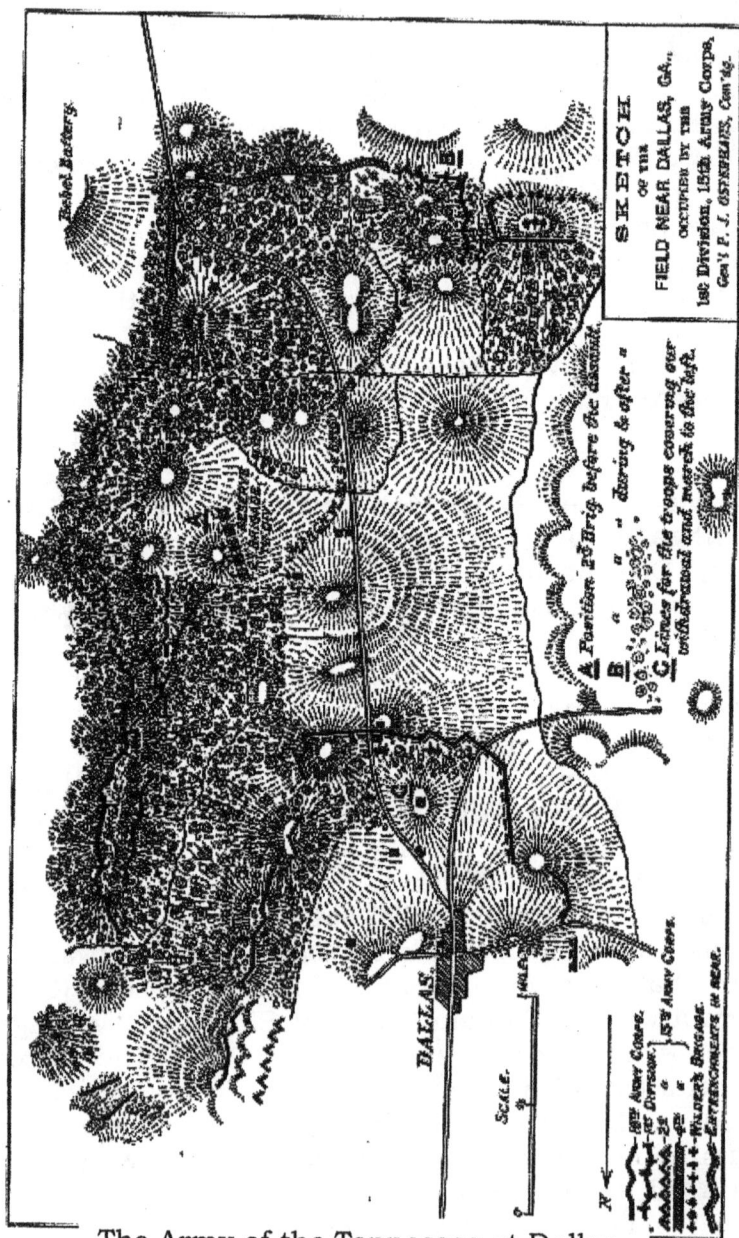

The Army of the Tennessee at Dallas

A particular concern to Logan was the position of Harrow's right flank, which ran along a ridge south of Dallas. Here the Union line crossed the Villa Rica Road, made a right-angle turn, and ended on a hill to the west of the Road. Brigadier General Charles Walcutt's (2nd) Brigade, holding the center of Harrow's line, faced east, with its right anchored on the Road. On Walcutt's right Colonel Ruben Williams' (1st) Brigade continued the line to the west, joining Wilder's Brigade. This area was considered "the weakest point in our whole position" by the 15th Corps commander, not only due to the salient here, but also because the ground in front of Harrow increased in height. "It had been considered impracticable," said Logan, "to carry our line far enough forward across this ridge to overcome this objectionable point, without weakening it [our line] too much elsewhere in thus adding to its length." 162 This sector invited a Confederate attack, and created a situation similar to that which concerned Thomas on the Federal left at Pickett's Mill.

Confederate dispositions in the Dallas Sector changed on May 27, due to "some advantage gained by the enemy to the right of Bate." This refers to a hill occupied by troops of Osterhaus' Federal Division during the night of May 26-27, which commanded the right of Bate's line. This "advantage" had been made possible due to the gap which existed between Bate's right and Cheatham's left. Bate made this known to Johnston, who ordered Cheatham's Division to join Bate's right and assist with the capture of the hill.163 However, Bate did not wait for Cheatham to arrive. At daylight on the 27th, four regiments from Brigadier General Joseph Lewis' and Smith's brigades attacked the Federals on the hill, (part of Colonel James Williamson's Brigade, Osterhaus' Division), "who fled from the boldness and rapidity of the move so rapidly as to forbid the capture of more than six or eight."

Cheatham's Division arrived soon after, and relieved
Bate's victorious troops.[164]   The Federals, however,
continued the contest later the same day, attacking the
20th Tennessee on this hill "a number of times, and at
one time the contestants fought across a rail pile about
4 feet through." [165]   Despite this effort the attack failed
to   dislodge   the   Tennesseeans,   and   the   position
remained in Confederate hands, becoming a significant
stronghold.

       To further strengthen the line in the Dallas area,
Walker's Division was moved from New Hope Church to
Bate's left.   On the same day as Bate's attack, these
new arrivals assaulted Walcutt's Brigade.   According
to Walcutt the proximity of the enemy line (500 yards
away),   augmented   by   one   of   the   two   Confederate
batteries previously mentioned, made his position "a
difficult one."   The Confederate attack was preceded by
an   artillery   shelling   about   1   p.m.,   followed   by   the
infantry   assault.   The   103rd   Illinois,   deployed   as
skirmishers in front of Walcutt's line, were the first to
receive the Confederate attack.   Captain Charles Wills,
commanding a portion of the skirmish line, described
the rebels as "jumping along through the brush . . .
making the bullets rain among us."   Wills' men were
forced back by the Confederates into the main line.[166]

       At   one   point   in   this   fight,   the   Confederates
gained a significant piece of ground, forcing Walcutt to
advance   the   6th   Iowa   (Lieutenant   Colonel   Alexander
Miller),   "which   they   did   most   gallantly,   meeting   the
enemy with bayonets fixed."   Walcutt continued: "The
fight   soon   became   general   along   my   front.   The   men
reserved their fire handsomely until the enemy's line
reached   the   base   of   the   hill,   when   they   opened,
scattering and driving the enemy with great loss."   At
one point the 8th Mississippi (John Jackson's Brigade),
threatened to flank Walcutt's right, but was stopped by
Miller's regiment, which refused its line under fire and

repulsed the Confederate attack.[167]   Although serious enough, this engagement was but a shower compared to the storm which would break in the same sector the next day.

No further significant action occurred on the 27th, other than the ever-present skirmishing. During the night a significant Confederate re-deployment took place with the shift of Cheatham's and Walker's Divisions back to the right. These troops were ordered to occupy the line to the right of Bate vacated by Polk's Corps, which was in turn ordered to the extreme Confederate right flank as part of a planned Confederate attack there. Bate's Division remained in position, holding the line east of Dallas, while Jackson's Cavalry Division occupied the extreme left south of the town.[168]

Chapter 8   **The Battle of Dallas**
                        "Everything spoke the sharp notes of war"

During the morning of May 28, having the higher ground in the Dallas sector, Johnston was able to observe the Federals moving their supply trains northeast.   Concluding that Sherman was attempting to shift his army to the left, the Confederate commander determined to catch the Federals while they were evacuating their lines in the Dallas sector. He therefore issued the following order to Bate in that area: "General Johnston desires you to develop the enemy, ascertain his strength and position, as it is believed he is not in force."   The order was received by Bate "during the afternoon," and "was in keeping with my own [Bate's] opinion and that of General Jackson." [169]   Bate's plan to effect Johnston's order directed Jackson   to move one brigade (Brigadier General Samuel W. Ferguson's) of cavalry to the Van Wert Road, west of Dallas and beyond the Federal right flank. To the right (east) of Ferguson, Brigadier General Frank Armstrong's Cavalry Brigade was ordered to attack directly forward, north, along the Villa Rica Road to Dallas.   Ross' Brigade was to move to a position southwest of Dallas, between Ferguson and Armstrong. On Armstrong's right Bate's infantry brigades (deployed left to right) of   Smith, Finley and Lewis (the "Orphan Brigade") would attack in echelon after Armstrong, at a signal from Cobb's artillery.   The signal would only be

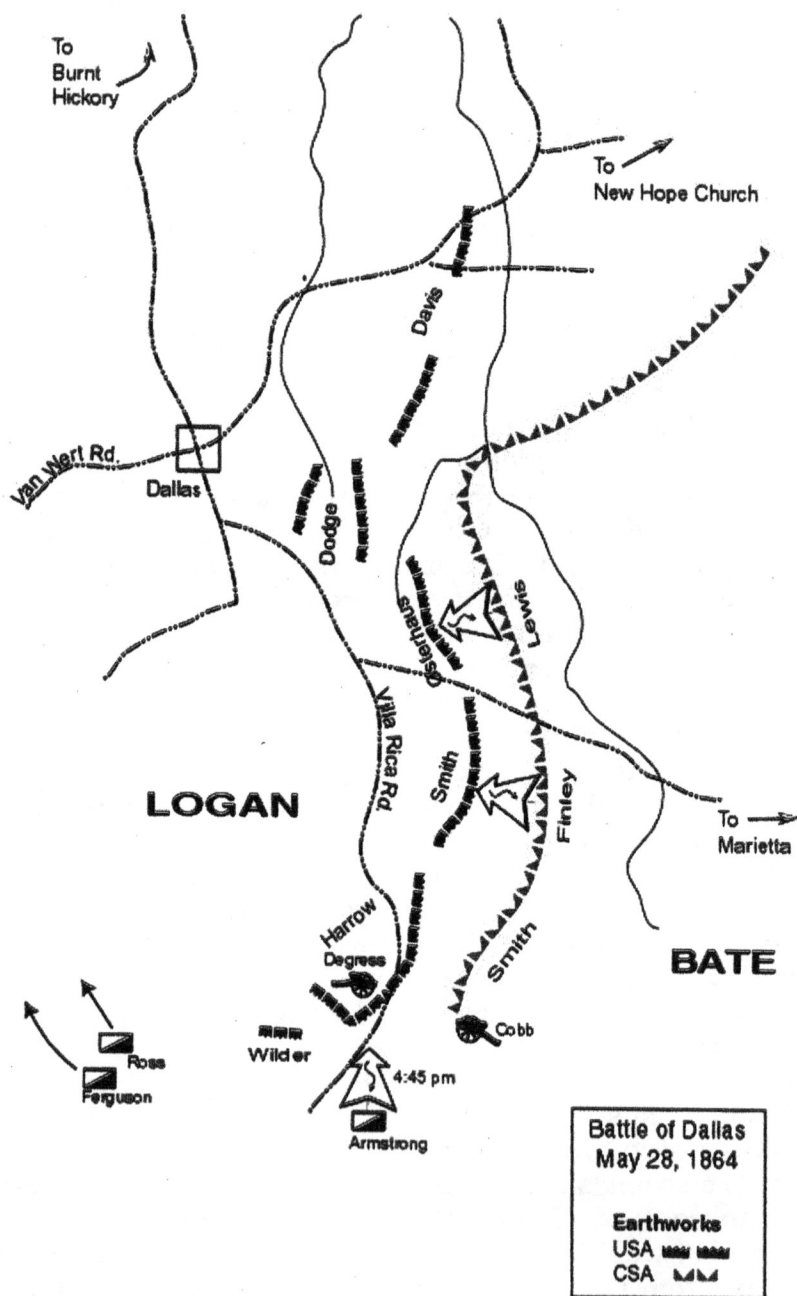

To
Burnt
Hickory

To
New Hope Church

Davis

Van Wert Rd.

Dallas

Dodge

Lewis

Osterhaus

Villa Rica Rd.

Smith

Finley

LOGAN

To
Marietta

Harrow

Smith

Degress

BATE

Ross

Wilder

Cobb

Ferguson

4:45 pm

Armstrong

Battle of Dallas
May 28, 1864

Earthworks
USA ▬▬ ▬▬
CSA ▼▼▼

given if Armstrong encountered little or no Federal
resistance. When opposition ceased, each unit was to
execute a right wheel realigning the front to the North,
perpendicular to the anticipated Federal line. Bate held
a meeting of his commanders to make sure they
understood the plan.

This "development" attack began, by
McPherson's account, at 4:45 p.m. General Armstrong
soon found that the Federals had not withdrawn, as
anticipated, but were "in force and entrenched". [170] If
the attack had gone as planned, it would have ended
with Armstrong's withdrawal at this point. However,
Armstrong's dismounted cavalry got so embroiled in
their assault that they were unable to quickly extricate
themselves. Hearing the prolonged sound of heavy
musketry and artillery firing to their left, Bullock
(Finley) and Lewis concluded that the signal must have
been given, but not heard, so they promptly ordered
their troops to join the attack. Smith's Brigade, closest
to Armstrong and thus close to the "signal station"
(Cobb's artillery), did not hear the signal and thus did
not attack.[171] John Jackman, in the 9th Kentucky of
the Orphan Brigade, recalled the charge: "We took off
all extra baggage, so that we would not be encumbered
in any way, and waited the word. Soon the musketry
and artillery commenced to roar in the valley to our left
and front, and the mingling yells of our boys charging
was plainly heard. The firing lasted only a few minutes,
then became perfectly silent - we knew the division had
been driven back, for soon after, our neighbors
[Federals] commenced cheering all around the lines." [172]
The 9th Kentucky, being on the right of the brigade
line, did not go forward due to the failure of the other
regiments in executing the right wheel. On Lewis' left
Finley's Brigade went forward far enough to encounter
Federal fire (from M. L. Smith's Division), but soon
received an order recalling the troops. Thus, of all

Bate's infantry, the Orphans, being the farthest away from Cobb's artillery, suffered the worst. This was due not only to the communication problem, but also to their having no support on the left flank after Finley withdrew. Several of the regiments on that end, particularly the 4th Kentucky, received enfilading fire from the Federals on their left.

It is commonly asserted that Lewis' Brigade lost 51% of its men in this attack. However, A. D. Kirwan in *Johnny Green of the Orphan Brigade*, contends (p. 133) that Green's 51% figure was exaggerated, and the loss was much lower: less than 10%. Kirwan bases this statement on the *Official Records* report submitted by A. J. Foard, the Army of Tennessee's Medical Director, covering "engagements near New Hope Church". Therefore, if one assumes that Foard's numbers are correct, the 20 killed and 177 wounded reported for Lewis' Brigade are the most the Orphans could have suffered.[173] This would also agree with General Bate's count (see page 84).

Another reason for Lewis' disproportionate loss was the defense of Osterhaus' (1st) Division, which had not withdrawn, and was fully prepared. Osterhaus himself was not present at the outset of Lewis' attack, but had left the front to lead his Second brigade to reinforce the Federal right, where Armstrong's attack fell. In Osterhaus' absence, Brigadier General Charles Woods (1st Brigade) assumed command and directed the alignment of his own unit, plus that of Colonel Hugo Wangelin, the Third Brigade commander. These two units (Third Brigade on the right, First on the left), with the four Napoleons of the 4th Ohio battery (Captain George Froehlich) in the center, delivered the devastating fire to the attacking Kentuckians. Woods, in his official report, recalled the attack: "A general discharge of fire-arms from the rifle-pits commenced. The enemy's line soon wavered, rallied, wavered, and then disappeared, leaving their dead and severely wounded behind. So hasty was their retreat that some of the skirmishers of the Third Brigade, who were taken prisoners on their [Confederate] advance, were overlooked, and thus escaped. The nearest approach to any part of the line . . .was in that part of the Third Brigade held by the Third Missouri volunteers, where a few of the enemy advanced to within about twenty yards of the rifle-pits." Woods reported the attack lasted about 30 minutes.[174]

On the Union right, where the initial Confederate attack by Armstrong's Brigade was delivered, Harrow's Division was under pressure. These Federals had already repelled an attack the day before, and were thus well-aware of the Confederate attraction to their sector. Prior to the attack, the Confederate artillery opposite Harrow's men continued to harass them, despite the efforts of DeGress' counter-battery fire. Early in the afternoon Captain Griffith, 1st Iowa Battery, attempted to counteract the Confederate cannons by moving three of his guns to higher ground 150 yards beyond the main line, a risky move under the circumstances, as Dan Sickles could testify. Also like Gettysburg, this position was directly in the path of the Confederate planned assault. Soon after Griffith's guns began firing, Armstrong began his attack, striking Harrow's Second Brigade (Walcutt) at the Villa Rica Road, and threatening to capture the 1st Iowa's isolated guns. The Confederates surged forward, quickly surrounded the cannons, and drove back the Federal defenders.

Fortunately for Harrow's men, General Logan had already sent a message to Osterhaus, ordering his Second Brigade (Williamson) to be sent immediately. When the courier arrived in the rear of Osterhaus' Division, he found Williamson's Brigade in formation, ready to move, led by Osterhaus himself, who had anticipated the order! These troops quickly followed the courier back to Harrow's front. The 6th Iowa (Walcutt's brigade), having saved the day previously, also surged forward and, together with Osterhaus' men, charged the Confederates and retook the guns. Nearby the 46th Ohio, armed with Spencer 7-shot repeaters, poured their deadly fire into Armstrong's ranks. Captain Wills, of the 103rd Illinois, recounted the crisis of this fight: "When the musketry was playing the hottest [Major General John] Logan came dashing up along our line, waved his hat and told the boys to 'give them hell, boys.' You should have heard them cheer him." [175] Two Federal commanders, Colonel Dickerman, commander of the 103rd Illinois, and Major Giesy, 46th Ohio, both of the Second Brigade, were killed in this action. Giesy had been a friend of the Sherman family since 1862. Farther along the front of the Second Brigade, Colonel Walcutt disdained the enemy fire and "stood on the parapet, amid the storm of bullets, ruling the fight." [176]

This stubborn resistance and heavy Federal counter-attack was too much for Armstrong's single brigade who, it will be remembered, was to withdraw under such circumstances, but found this task difficult to achieve. On Armstrong's right, the brief Confederate attack by Finley's Brigade on M. L. Smith's (2nd) Division was met with the same determination. Thomas Taylor, a member of Smith's headquarters staff, remembered the attack in this area: "A most terrific storm broke over our lines and came rolling on toward us - demonic yells were the intruders - The enemy was charging. . . . Our artillery belched forth its fierce thunders and our rifles emitted one continuous sheet of flame and lead, reserves were hurrying, and everything spoke the sharp notes of war." Fortunately for Finley's Brigade, the order for withdrawal came soon.[177]

On the extreme right of the Union line west of the Villa Rica Road, similar results were reported. Lieutenant Colonel James Goodnow (1st Brigade, 12th Indiana), saw the Confederates press forward in his front "to within 200 yards of my works, where they attempted to reform their broken lines. The attempt proved unsuccessful, as they were so much exposed to my fire, and which eventually drove them from the field." [178]   Still further to the right, Wilder's Brigade added its Spencer rifle fire into Armstrong's ranks.

Based on the Federal accounts, it would seem that Armstrong's attack achieved much more than expected (or ordered).   It drew the attention of two complete Federal brigades, plus portions of two others. While the placing of three guns beyond the main line gave Armstrong an advantage, the primary explanation for the brief Confederate success in this area comes from two factors. First, General Bate's attack plan did not include a preliminary artillery bombardment, which usually preceded an assault, and was intended to soften up the enemy line. This tactic seldom achieved the desired effect, however, but rather worked against the attackers by alerting the defender to the impending action.   Since the Union line was expected to be abandoned or lightly held, Bate probably did not consider a barrage, hoping to achieve some surprise, as well as prevent the Federals from reinforcing their position. General Logan had correctly anticipated the second cause of Confederate success: the critical high ground on Harrow's front. It not only provided cover for the attackers, but it was also too great a temptation for Captain Griffith![179]

Losses in this battle are, as usual, easier to tally for the Union than the Confederates. Logan reported a total of 379, with 97 Confederate prisoners captured. He estimated 2,000 Confederate casualties, and mentions the burial of over 300 Confederate bodies.

This estimate varies significantly with Confederate records which lists Bate's Division as suffering a total of 392 killed and wounded for *all actions on the Dallas line*. Adding the 97 prisoners reported by Logan yields a total of 489 total losses for Bate's Division. Bate himself reports a total for *all Dallas Line actions* of 450 (62K, 314W, 74M). This does not include Armstrong's losses, for which there are no figures. Given this fact and that much of the earlier fighting in the Dallas area was quite severe, a figure of 400 for the Confederates is reasonable.[180]

Due to the communication difficulties encountered in the battle, as well as the losses in Lewis' Brigade, General Bate felt obliged to justify his actions. His assumption that McPherson was not holding his line in force was based in part on the lack of a Federal effort to retake the hill captured on the morning of the 27th. Bate also justified his signal-plan by explaining that Lewis had made an honest mistake when he ordered the Orphans to attack; after waiting for the signal longer than he anticipated, Lewis sent an officer to the left to investigate. Arriving at the position of Smith's Brigade, finding it vacant, and at the same time hearing the sound of Armstrong's attack, this officer concluded that the signal had been given but not heard by Lewis. The officer therefore returned to Lewis and reported that Smith had gone forward and that the Orphans were late. Actually, said Bate, Smith had formed in battleline and moved forward slightly in order to make the most effective attack, if required. Thus, according to Bate, the "ardor of [Lewis'] men could not be restrained, " and no blame was due to anyone. This explanation was accepted by Johnny Green, who justified the mistake as part of "the game of war". Lewis apparently felt otherwise, insisting that he was ordered to take the Federal works.[181]

General McPherson reported to Sherman after the battle that a Confederate attack was "handsomely repulsed, with heavy loss on his side and considerable on ours." He used this fact to argue against the shift left: "Unless an imperative necessity demands it, I do not see how I can move to-night ; besides, the effect on our men will be bad." Sherman agreed with McPherson, and the plan to withdraw the Army of the Tennessee on the night of May 28 was canceled.[182]

The "Lightening Bug" Battle

No major action beyond normal skirmishing occurred in the Dallas sector during the day of May 29. That night however, a significant combat began about 9 or 10 p.m., and, in some areas, lasted all night. Although never reaching "battle" proportions, this nocturnal firefight illustrates the tension felt by both sides, and therefore deserves mention. Typically for an action of this nature, it is difficult to determine its origin. In this case an account from Johnny Green (Lewis' Brigade) serves well: "The Florida boys [Finley's Brigade] on pickets mistook the flash of the lightning bug for the flash of a yankee gun and fired at the flash. The ball wizzed over the head of the yankee picket who in turn fired and this started the firing which grew rapidly at every flash." Bate supports Green's account with a report of a Union attack at 11 p.m. on his right, which drove in his skirmishers, but got no further. However, recalls Bate, heavy artillery and musketry continued at intervals until dawn.[183] Jackman also remembers this night battle, that woke him from his "slumbers". He quickly rushed to the trenches and saw "a perfect sheet of flame coming over the enemy's works, and the flash of cannon lit up the dark woods so we could see the cannoneers quite plain. . . . We thought we saw a line advancing up the hill, and opened fire. . . . Cleburne thought our division [was] attacked, and came to reinforce us [with Govan's Brigade]." [184]   Captain Irving Buck of Cleburne's Division also adds his testimony: "It was ascertained later that a false rumor of the Confederates advancing caused this firing." [185]   Union reports of this "battle" support Bate's assertion that it occurred on his right, the Union 16th Corps' front. However, General Dodge, who had been occupied during the day with the withdrawal of his supply trains, reported that he was the *defender* in this fight: the Confederates "in heavy columns assaulted my lines, making five separate determined attacks." So severe was this attack that it caused the postponement of the 16th Corps' withdrawal. Dodge's subordinates also mentioned this battle, although the assaults were reported by Sweeny as "demonstrations". Farther along the Federal line, units of M. L. Smith's Division (15th Corps) described "a general attack by the enemy on our entire line." [186]

While it is easy for soldiers to imagine more at night than at other times, it seems certain that the action on Dodge's front increased beyond the usual level of night skirmishes. Johnny Green recalled that after this engagement, whenever they met Finley's Brigade, they called out, "Boys we will get you some blacking to blacken the lightening bugs lamps, for we don't want you to bring on any more night attacks." [187]

Chapter 9   **Pickett's Mill, Reprise**
"Will endeavor to gain ground to our left"

A May 29 proposed action at Pickett's Mill is the substance of one of the many episodes in the dispute that arose between Hood and Johnston regarding the conduct of the campaign.   Essentially, Hood proposed to Johnston an attack on the Union left flank, to begin on the morning of May 29, using Hood's whole Corps; Johnston agreed. This plan was based on information Hood had received from Wheeler that the Federal position east of Pickett's Mill Creek was vulnerable.   It is at this point that the participant's accounts of the incident disagree. Johnston reported that during a "usual" meeting of the Lieutenant Generals on May 28, Hood put forward the idea of attacking the Federal left. Johnston agreed and gave orders to the other Lieutenant Generals to support Hood's plan. It was to be a general engagement with Hood beginning the attack, followed down the line to his left, in succession, by Polk's and Hardee's troops. In essence it was identical to what Howard had attempted two days earlier in the same place! About 10 a.m. the next day, according to Johnston, a message was received from Hood reporting that the Federal left was refused, entrenched, not open to attack, and requesting further instructions. The Army Commander, assuming that Hood was in the presence of the enemy, decided that the delay caused by Hood's request for instructions would result not only in the loss of surprise, but also the addition of Federal reinforcements to the threatened area.   Johnston therefore called off the attack. He later discovered that Hood's troops had been marched 8 to 10 hours to reach a point six miles from the Union flank, "which was little more than a musket-shot from his starting point." [188]

Hood's account of this incident is, predictably, completely different. According to Hood, the plan was first proposed to Johnston, who then called the meeting of the Lieutenant Generals. Hood said the attack was based on Wheeler's report that "the enemy had its left flank beyond [east] this [Little Pumpkinvine] stream, in a position which was exposed by reason of the difficulty of passage back to the main body of their Army." In Hood's view the attack was to be carried out only if "the enemy's left flank remain[ed] as represented." He further stated that as his troops approached the objective at dawn, May 29, he received a message saying that he "need proceed no further, as the Federals had during the night, drawn back their left flank, re-crossed Little Pumpkinvine Creek, and were entrenched [on the west side]." [189]

To resolve these conflicting accounts, two sources should be considered. First, the "Journal of the First Brigade", Carlin's (First Division, 14th Corps), records that on the morning of May 28, his men "advanced [from their May 27 position east of the creek] about one-quarter of a mile and the brigade was formed in single line extending from right to left along the ridge in front of Leverett's and Brand's houses. About 3 p.m. the 1st Wisconsin (Third brigade) [Scribner's] was put in position on the right of the brigade, *to complete the line to Pumpkin Vine Creek.*" (emphasis added) Leverett's and Brand's houses were less than 1/4 mile east of Pickett's Mill Creek. Colonel Scribner, whose brigade was behind King's early on the 28th, reported that Carlin's line "moved up on the left [east] of the creek, on a line with General King." It can be inferred from these two accounts that King's left rested on Pickett's Mill Creek. The goal of all these movements was to *reinforce* the Union position east of the stream. There is no mention in the reports of these units of a withdrawal, as Hood contends, back to the west side of the stream at any time.[190]

Another source, Lieutenant T. B. Mackall's journal entry for May 28, also contradicts Hood's assertion that the Federals had withdrawn to the west side of the creek: "Hood found enemy's right on Allatoona Road entrenched." [191] This road was *east* of Pickett's Mill Creek. Mackall states further that Hood's Corps had, at sunrise, not crossed to the east side of the stream, which agrees with Hood's account. Given that Hood's troops were so far away from their objective, an attack as proposed would have been difficult to carry out without alerting the Union troops. Thus, as at Cassville, a planned Confederate attack was not carried out, leaving Hood and Johnston blaming each other for the failure.

Despite this, Confederate interest in the Union left flank continued, and on May 31, Hood launched a probing attack against the Federals on both sides of Pickett's Mill Creek. These were the troops of Wood's (3rd) and Johnson's (1st) Division, recently participants in the Battle of Pickett's Mill, now dug in on high ground, respectively to the west and east of Pickett's Mill Creek. Johnson at this time comprised the left flank of the Union infantry line, in the vicinity of the Brand house. Hood asked for and received the cooperation of Major General William Loring's Division (of Polk's Corps).

The purpose of this action was to "ascertain whether the enemy were in our front in force";

consequently the entire attack was by skirmish lines from the two Corps. Loring's troops were from Brigadier General Winfield Featherston's and Brigadier General Thomas Scott's brigades, positioned on Hood's right, east of the creek. Hood supplied skirmishers from Hindman's Division, west of Pickett's Mill Creek. These Confederates advanced a few hundred yards and struck the first Union skirmish line. On Loring's front this line was overrun, but the Confederates got no further due to heavy fire from the next Federal line. Having accomplished their mission, and losing 130 casualties in the process, they withdrew.[192]

Sergeant George Puntenney, a soldier of the 37th Indiana (Scribner's Brigade), recorded an enlightening account of this engagement; it reveals the tenacity typical of soldiers on both sides:

> All at once the firing on our left became very fierce, and it was evident the firing was done by the enemy. Then we saw our line of battle break and run like arrant [sic] cowards. Our hearts almost melted within us. Soon, we supposed, the enemy would swing around and pour an enfilading fire on us, and the battle and bloodshed would be fearful. Just then we saw our soldiers returning to their places as fast as they could run. They got back to their position and soon drove back the rebel forces. Never in all my life did I love Union soldiers as I did those. They had left their guns behind and gone forward to intrench themselves, and when attacked, ran back for their guns, got them and held their position. Good, brave fellows that they were![193]

While Sherman had successfully avoided Confederate attempts to flank him on both ends of his line, he was still short of his immediate goal, shifting the Army of the Tennessee to his left. In a telegram to Halleck the morning of May 29, the Federal commander reported the Battle of Dallas: the Confederates were repulsed "with great slaughter" and their loss estimated at 2,500. In regard to moving McPherson's Army he said, "I give him to-day (Sunday) to gather in the wounded and bury the dead of both sides, and to night and to-morrow will endeavor to gain ground to our left three or four miles. . . . I have no doubt Johnston has in my front every man he can scrape." [194]

It was not until the night of May 31, however, that the Army of the Tennessee finally began its move, the majority of McPherson's troops moving cautiously on June 1. They took up a position from the vicinity of Owen's Mill to New Hope Church, and relieved Hooker's Corps, which moved to the Army of the Cumberland's left, east of Pickett's Mill and near the Allatoona Road. Schofield's troops were moved to Thomas' left, where they joined Hooker. This extended the Federal Line substantially and threatened the Confederate right flank.[195] Garrard's and Stoneman's cavalry were sent to escort the trains, and to capture Allatoona Pass. Stoneman took Allatoona Pass on June 1 without opposition. "Thus the real object of my move on Dallas was accomplished," Sherman said, although as an anti-climax to the events of the past week, and likely costing more time than he anticipated.[196]

During these movements, Johnston reverted to the defensive, and prepared to match the Federal shift. Hardee's Corps was reunited with the transfer of Cleburne's Division from the right (May 29). On June 1, as the Federal northeast-ward shift became apparent, Cleburne was moved again, this time from Hardee's left-center to the New Hope Church area and placed in reserve. The Confederate line by June 1 consisted of Hardee's Corps on the left, holding Ray and

Elsberry's Mountains, Polk's Corps in the center, at New Hope Church, and Hood on the right, in the vicinity of Pickett's Mill. Wheeler's Cavalry was on Hood's right, holding the Allatoona Road, facing McCook's Federals.[197]

The same day, Confederates of Bate's and Jackson's Divisions discovered the abandoned Federal works in the Dallas sector. John Jackman recounted the scene: "I walked around their works which are very strong. Nothing left but beef bones, and empty ammunition boxes. Some places the bushes in front of their works are literally mown down by minie balls - done on the night of the 29th May, I presume; and, when our brigade charged on the 28th." [198]

At this point in the Atlanta Campaign, a significant weather change occurred, recorded by Rice Bull in his diary: "On May 25th the weather changed and I find . . . that for twenty-one days it stormed every day. . . .It was such a time of great activity that these storms either caught us on the march or in breastworks where we had no protection. After one of these rains the men would be as wet as if they had fallen in a stream. . . . Our trains were well up in front but could only be moved with great difficulty." [199]

This incessant rain actually began in earnest on June 1, and would, until he reached the Kennesaw Line later in the month, severely hamper Sherman's movements, slowing the progress of the Campaign. From the beginning on May 7, to the Dallas Line, a period of roughly three weeks, the Federals had advanced over ninety miles into Georgia. It would take them another *month* to move the ten miles from Dallas to Marietta. While the rain was not the only factor in affecting Sherman's progress, it was highly significant, and would have its effect on the next Federal movements on the Dallas Line.

Chapter 10   The Battle of Foster's Farm
"Change without further battle"

The focus of the Campaign now shifted to the Federal left, where Sherman endeavored to re-join the railroad at Acworth. Sherman's shifting had placed Schofield's and Hooker's Corps on the Federal left, threatening the Burnt Hickory-Allatoona Road junction. If this crucial point was captured, Sherman's Army would threaten the Confederate right flank while at the same time open the way to Acworth.

On June 2, Johnston re-deployed his army to counter the Federal shift to the right, just in time to stop Sherman's next thrust. Hardee's Corps, minus Cheatham's Division, was moved to the right of Hood, protecting the Burnt Hickory-Allatoona crossroads, near the Foster house. The Confederate line was thus arranged with Cheatham's Division holding the left near New Hope Church, followed left to right by Polk's, Hood's, and Hardee's Corps. Wheeler remained on the Confederate right, in the vicinity of Allatoona Church, still confronting McCook.[200]

During the afternoon on June 2, Schofield's troops advanced east along the Burnt Hickory Road, Hovey's Division on the right, Cox's in the center, and Hascall's Division on the left. Moving through dense underbrush and a heavy thunderstorm, they approached Allatoona Creek, where they were assailed by the artillery fire from Confederate works just to the east at the Foster house. Pressing back the Confederate skirmishers, Cox's Division struck the line of Armstrong's (dismounted) cavalry brigade, who, according to Cox, "were found to be strongly entrenched." Continuing with Cox's account, "The Second Division (Hascall) at this time was in rear of by left in echelon . . . and General Hascall, at my request, promptly moved his line forward to my support, swinging his left still further forward and nearer to the enemy's works, in hope of taking them in flank. " However, due to the rain and Confederate resistance, further advance was deemed impracticable, so Hascall's and Cox's men hastily dug in.[201]

Schofield's attack was to be closely supported by Butterfield's Division of Hooker's Corps, but due to an apparent disagreement, Butterfield did not advance when requested by Schofield. Butterfield's contention was that "although not in accordance with orders, I determined to do so [advance] as soon as directed; darkness came on before it could be done." This lack of cooperation between Schofield and Butterfield perhaps cost the Federals a victory in the Battle of Foster's Farm that day. A Union capture of the critical road intersection could have had severe consequences for the Confederates.[202]

The Battle here was concluded the next day, June 3, when Schofield ordered Hovey's Division from his right to the left. Moving again through rain, Hovey's men struggled through the woods under Confederate fire to Allatoona Church, which they secured by sundown. They were soon reinforced by other troops, and now held a strong position beyond the Confederate right flank. This action precipitated an immediate Confederate withdrawal from the whole Dallas Line, on the night of June 3-4, and ended that phase of the

campaign.[203]   Having previously selected his next
position, Johnston fell back to the Lost Mountain Line,
about three miles to the rear, in Cobb County. Here the
contest would shortly be resumed.[204]

Sherman summarized the end of the Dallas Line
operations in his memoirs: "On the 4th of June I was
preparing to draw off from New Hope Church, and to
take position on the railroad in front of Allatoona,
when, General Johnston himself having evacuated his
position, we effected the change without further battle."
The Federal commander related to his wife that
"[Johnston] thinks he checked us at Dallas. I went
there to avoid the Allatoona Pass, and as soon as I had
drawn his Army there I Slipped my Cavalry into
Allatoona Pass & moved the main army in its front a
perfect success. I never designed to attack his hastily
prepared works at Dallas and New Hope Church, and
as soon as he saw I was making for the Railroad around
his Right flank he abandoned his works and we
occupied them for a moment and moved by the best
Roads to our present position [south of Acworth]." [205]
This last statement is true in part: the Federal
commander did turn Johnston out of his Allatoona
position. However, Sherman denies his opponent a
significant success: blocking the Union effort to cut the
railroad at Marietta. It was this potential victory which
helped to weigh the scale in favor of the side-step into
Paulding County.

Chapter 11

Conclusion
"Moving on the vigorous offensive"

There had surely been enough battle to this point. Casualties, although in Sherman's words "impossible to state accurately . . . in any one separate battle," can be approximated from military reports as 4,000 Union, 3,000 Confederate. Confederate losses are, in this case, reported separately for the Dallas Line as 276 killed and 1729 wounded, totaling 2,005. Wheeler's Cavalry reported for the month of May 73 killed, 341 wounded. Jackson's Cavalry did not make a report. Dividing Wheeler's numbers by four (one week) gives an approximate loss on the Dallas Line of 20 killed and 85 wounded, for a combined total for the Army of Tennessee (minus Jackson) of 2110 (296 killed, 1814 wounded). This figure does not account for prisoners, however. Using Sherman's total of Confederate prisoners for May (3245), and dividing by four to give an approximate weekly total, yields 800. Adding this figure to the killed/wounded number gives a grand total of about 3000. Federal losses can be estimated by totaling the casualties reported in the three battles: New Hope Church, Pickett's Mill, and Dallas. Combining these figures yields a total of 3645. Adding for losses due to the extremely severe skirmishing and smaller engagements for which totals were not reported, would give an approximate Union loss of 4,000 for the Dallas Line (May 23 - June 3).[206]

Was this "bill" worth the effort in by-passing the Confederate's Allatoona position? As already seen, Sherman felt that his goals had been achieved. In addition to avoiding a confrontation at Allatoona, he had hoped to lure the Confederate Army out of its fortifications, where it could be defeated. Despite his acting "with reasonable caution . . . moving on the vigorous offensive," the terrain in Paulding County made any Union victory very difficult, influencing the Confederates as well, at Dallas on May 28th and in the planned assault at Pickett's Mill on the 29th.[207] While these attempts failed, they serve as a sign of another change in the military situation: the terrain had more than offset Sherman's diminished strength advantage, and allowed Johnston the opportunity to make offensive moves. These factors resulted in the Federal Commander's inability to pin his adversary on the Dallas Line and quickly outflank him. On the contrary, Sherman was only able to do so when, after a four-day struggle, he extricated McPherson's Army from Confederate clutches in the Dallas area.

Even if the Federals had been able to use their previously successful tactic of hold and flank, one essential element was missing: there was no railroad in the immediate Confederate rear. This was an advantage for Johnston; he did not have to fear a threat to his supply line, and could assume a more aggressive posture. On the other hand, Sherman's options were limited by his lack of a rail line nearby, and therefore could not maneuver wherever he wished. Johnston was aware of this limitation, and attempted to take advantage of it in the attack at Dallas on the 28th.

Since defeating the Confederate Army outside its Allatoona position had proved so difficult, would

Sherman have done just as well by forging ahead along the railroad? Had Sherman pressed on against the Confederate position at Allatoona, he would first have had to get across the river against Confederate opposition, then drive Johnston out of his mountain fortifications. While the first part of this task proved not so difficult, the second may well have been costly. Despite the easy crossing of the Etowah at Stilesboro, Johnston still held a strong north-south line along Pumpkinvine Creek, near its junction with the River. This would have prevented a flanking maneuver similar to that used by the Union at Resaca. Knowing the Allatoona area as he did, it is no wonder Sherman avoided what he was sure would be a difficult obstacle and chose to take his chances in Paulding County. This gamble paid off by forcing the Confederate army out of a formidable position; it had the potential to yield a more substantial victory by cutting Johnston's supply line at Marietta. Since these 'end runs' had born fruit before, Sherman believed it was possible again – his sojourn in the "Hell Hole" was well worth the cost.

Atlanta Campaign Order of Battle
Taken from *Official Records*, edited to reflect Dallas Line assignments.

UNION
MILITARY DIVISION OF THE MISSISSIPPI (Sherman)

Army of the Cumberland (Thomas)

IV Army Corps (Howard)

1st Division (Stanley)
1st Division Artillery
(Simonson)

1st Brigade (Cruft)
2nd Brigade (Whitaker)
3rd Brigade (Grose)

2nd Division (Newton)
2nd Division Artillery
(Aleshire)

1st Brigade (Kimball)
2nd Brigade (Wagner)
3rd Brigade (Harker)

3rd Division (Wood)
3rd Division Artillery
(Bradley)

1st Brigade (Gibson)
2nd Brigade (Hazen)
3rd Brigade (Knefler)

XIV Army Corps (Palmer)

1st Division (Johnson)
1st Division Artillery
(Drury)

1st Brigade (Carlin)
2nd Brigade (King)
3rd Brigade (Scribner)

2nd Division (Davis)

2nd Division Artillery
(Barnett)

1st Brigade (Morgan)
2nd Brigade (Mitchell)
3rd Brigade (McCook)

3rd Division (Baird)
[Guarding wagon trains at Burnt Hickory]

XX Army Corps (Hooker)

1st Division (Williams)
1st Division Artillery
(Woodbury)

1st Brigade (Knipe)
2nd Brigade (Ruger)
3rd Brigade (Robinson)

2nd Division (Geary)
2nd Division Artillery
(Wheeler)

1st Brigade (Candy)
2nd Brigade (Lockman)
3rd Brigade (Cobham)

3rd Division (Butterfield)
3rd Division Artillery
(Gary)

1st Brigade (Ward)
2nd Brigade (Coburn)
3rd Brigade (Wood)

Cavalry Corps (Elliott)

1st Division (McCook)

1st Brigade (Dorr)
2nd Brigade (Lamson)
3rd Brigade [Refitting at
Chattanooga]

2nd Division (Garrard)

1st Brigade (Minty)
2nd Brigade [Operating in
northern Alabama]
3rd Brigade (Wilder)

3rd Division (Lowe)
[Assigned to Kingston,
Georgia]

Army of the Ohio (Schofield)

XXIII Army Corps (Schofield)

1st Division (Hovey)
1st Division Artillery
(commander not
mentioned)

1st Brigade (Barter)

2nd Brigade (McQuiston)
2nd Division (Hascall)
2nd Division Artillery
(Shields)

1st Brigade (McLean)

2nd Brigade (Bond)
3rd Brigade (Strickland)
3rd Division (Cox)
3rd Division Artillery
(Wells)

1st Brigade (Reilly)
2nd Brigade (Casement)
3rd Brigade (McLean)

Stoneman's Cavalry Division
1st Brigade (Garrard)
2nd Brigade (Biddle)
3rd Brigade (Capron)
Independent Cavalry Brigade (Holeman)

Army of the Tennessee (McPherson)

XV Army Corps (Logan)

1st Division (Osterhaus)
1st Division Artillery
(Landgraeber)

1st Brigade (Woods)
2nd Brigade (Williamson)
3rd Brigade (Wangelin)

2nd Division (M.L. Smith)
(Artillery commander not mentioned)

1st Brigade (G.A. Smith)

2nd Brigade (Lightburn)

3rd Division (J. E. Smith)
[Assigned as railroad-guard, Cartersville, Georgia]

4th Division (Harrow)
4th Division Artillery
(Cheney)

1st Brigade (Williams)
2nd Brigade (Walcutt)
3rd Brigade (Oliver)

XVI Army Corps (Dodge)

2nd Division (Sweeny)
2nd Division Artillery
(Welker)

1st Brigade (Rice)
2nd Brigade (Mersy)

3rd Brigade (Bane)
[Assigned to garrison
Rome, Georgia]

4th Division (Veatch)
4th Division Artillery
(Burrows)

1st Brigade (Fuller)
2nd Brigade (Sprague)
3rd Brigade [In Decatur,
Alabama]

XVII Army Corps (Blair)
[Not present for Dallas Line action]

CONFEDERATE

Army of Tennessee (Johnston)

Hardee's Corps

Corps Artillery (Smith)

Hoxton's Battalion
Hotchkiss' Battalion
Martin's Battalion
Cobb's Battalion
Palmer's Battalion

Bate's Division

Finley's Brigade (Bullock)
Lewis' (Orphan) Brigade
Smith's Brigade

Cheatham's Division

Maney's Brigade
Strahl's Brigade
Vaughn's Brigade
Wright's Brigade (Carter)

Cleburne's Division
Govan's Brigade
Granbury's Brigade
Lowrey's Brigade
Polk's Brigade

Walker's Division

Gist's Brigade
Jackson's Brigade
Mercer's Brigade
Stevens' Brigade

Hood's Corps

Hood's Corps Artillery (Beckham)

Courtney's Battalion
Eldridge's Battalion
Johnston's Battalion (Van Den Corput)
Williams' Battalion

Hindman's Division

Deas' Brigade
Manigault's Brigade
Tucker's Brigade (Sharp)
Walthall's Brigade

Stewart's Division

Baker's Brigade

Clayton's Brigade
Gibson's Brigade
Stovall's Brigade (Johnson)

Stevenson's Division

Brown's Brigade
Cumming's Brigade
Pettus' Brigade
A. W. Reynolds' Brigade

Polk's Corps

Polk's Corps Artillery

Myrick's Battalion
Storr's Battalion
Preston's Battalion
Waddell's Battalion

French's Division

Cockrell's Brigade
Ector's Brigade
Sears' Brigade

Loring's Division

Adam's Brigade
Featherston's Brigade

Scott's Brigade

Walthall's Division

Cantey's Brigade
Quarles' Brigade
D.H. Reynolds' Brigade

Wheeler's Cavalry Corps

Horse Artillery

Robertson's Battalion
Jackson's Cavalry Division Artillery

Humes' Division

Ashby's Cavalry Brigade
Harrison's Cavalry Brigade

Jackson's Division

Armstrong's Cavalry Brigade
Ferguson's Cavalry Brigade
Ross' Cavalry Brigade

Kelly's Division

Anderson's Cavalry Brigade
Dibrell's Cavalry Brigade
Hannon's Cavalry Brigade
Williams' Cavalry Brigade

Martin's Division

Allen's Cavalry Brigade
Iverson's Cavalry Brigade

Endnotes

[1]Ambrose Bierce, "The Crime at Pickett's Mill," *Ambrose Bierce's Civil War* (Washington, D.C.: Regnery Gateway, 1956), p. 38.

[2]William T. Sherman, *Memoirs of General William T. Sherman, By Himself*, Vol. II (Indiana University Press, Civil War Centennial Series, 1957), p. 46.

[3]U.S. War Department, *The War of the Rebellion: The Official Records of the Union and Confederate Armies*, 128 vols. (Washington, D.C., 1890-1901), Series I, vol. 38, part I, p. 2. Hereinafter cited as *OR*. All references are to series I, Vol. 38 unless otherwise noted.

[4]Sherman's Army was composed of the Army of the Cumberland, Major General George Thomas commanding,

---

60,773 men; the Army of the Tennessee, Major General James

McPherson, 24,465; the Army of the Ohio, Major General John

Schofield, 13,559. Johnston's Army of Tennessee contained

Lieutenant General William Hardee's Corps, 21,947; Lieutenant

General John Hood's Corps, 21,310, and Major General

Joseph Wheeler's Cavalry Corps, 8,063. Lieutenant General

Leonidas Polk's Corps joined on June 11th with 21,547. These

are only the main elements of each army. It is essential in

counting troop strengths for the Atlanta Campaign that the

differences between Union & Confederate methods be

understood. The Union Army used "effective strength",

counting all men present for duty in any capacity. The

Confederates used a more complicated procedure, involving

the "effective total", which counted only those men in line

carrying muskets. OR, pt. I, p. 62-63; pt. III, p. 676-677; William R.

Scaife, The Campaign for Atlanta (4th ed. 1993), p. 9.

[5]OR, pt. III, p. 616; pt. IV, p. 736; Brooks D. Simpson and

Jean V. Berlin, ed. Sherman's Civil War, Selected

Correspondence of William T. Sherman, 1860-1865 (Chapel Hill:

University of North Carolina Press, 1999), p. 639.

    [6]OR, pt. I, p. 115; pt. III, p. 677; pt. IV, p. 373; Steven H. Newton, "Formidable Only in a Fight?" in *North and South Magazine* (vol.3, #4), p. 47. *The comparison is approximate, since Union returns are for May 31, and Confederate for June 10. The Union total of 103,000 is derived from the May 31 total minus the troops mentioned.*

    [7]OR, pt. II, p. 1

    [8]OR, pt. II, p. 1

    [9]3rd Brigade (Colonel Moses Bane), 2nd Division, 16th Corps

    [10]OR, pt. IV, pp. 274, 288

    [11]OR, pt. IV, p. 289

    [12]OR, pt. IV, pp. 291-292

    [13]The road between Dallas and Van Wert has the same name.

    [14]OR, pt. IV, p. 292

    [15]OR, pt. IV, p. 299

    [16]OR, pt. IV, p. 296

[17]OR, pt. II, p. 616, p. 766

[18]Sydney C. Kerksis, ed. *The Atlanta Papers* (Morningside Bookshop Press, 1980), p. 75.

[19]Kenneth W. Noe, ed., *A Southern Boy in Blue: The Memoir of Marcus Woodcock, 9th Kentucky Infantry* (Knoxville: University of Tennessee Press, 1996), p. 289.

[20]OR, pt. III, p. 704; A. D. Kirwan, ed. *Johnny Green of the Orphan Brigade, A Journal of a Confederate Soldier* (University of Kentucky Press: 1956), p. 131.

[21]OR,IV,731,737; Joseph E. Johnston, *Narrative of Military Operations During the Civil War* (New York: Da Capo Press, 1959), p. 325.

[22]OR, pt. III, pp. 616, 947; pt. IV, pp. 306,742. The reports of this action are difficult to reconcile. A Union officer reported 20 wagons captured and another 20 destroyed; Johnston reported 80 captured and 170 destroyed. Wheeler reported 70 or 80 wagons captured. A composite figure has been used here.

[23]*Narrative*, p. 350

[24]*OR*, pt. IV, p. 399.

[25]*OR*, pt. II, pp. 542,567,680.

[26]*OR*, pt. III, pp. 33,34; pt. IV, p. 305.

[27]*The Atlanta Papers*, p. 74.

[28]Arnold Gates, ed. *The Rough Side of War, the Civil War Journal of Chesley Mosman*. (Garden City: Basin Publishing Co., 1987), p.204.

[29]Letter from "Near Altoona, Ga., May 24th, 1864", Charles Harding Cox Papers, Emory University Special Collections, Atlanta, Ga.

[30]*OR*, pt. I, p. 143; pt. II, p. 812; pt. III, p. 252; pt. IV, p. 301.

[31]*OR*, pt. IV, p. 739.

[32]Zack C. Waters, ed. "The Partial Atlanta Reports of Confederate Maj. Gen. William B. Bate," in Theodore P. Savas and David A. Woodbury, ed. *The Campaign for Atlanta*, vol. I (Savas Woodbury Publishers, 1994), p. 209.

[33]*OR*, pt. III, p. 705.

[34]William C. Davis, ed., *Diary of a Confederate Soldier*,

John S. Jackman of the Orphan Brigade (University of South

Carolina Press, 1990), p. 129.

[35]O. O. Howard, "The Struggle for Atlanta," in _Battles

and Leaders of the Civil War_, vol. IV (Secaucus: Castle, 1982),

p. 306.

[36]_OR_, pt. IV, p. 308.

[37]_OR_, pt. II, p. 803; pt. III, p. 379; pt. IV, p. 308.

[38]_OR_, pt. II, pp. 542,567,680.

[39]_OR_, pt. II, p. 752.

[40]_OR_, pt. I, pp. 143, 862; pt. II, p. 29.

[41]Johnston, _Narrative_, p. 326.

[42]_OR_, pt. III, pp. 833,843.

[43]_OR_, pt. III, pp. 833, 843, 855.

[44]_Atlanta Papers_, 77-78; _OR_, pt. III, pp. 843-844, 862.

[45]Emphasis added; _Atlanta Papers_,78; _OR_, pt. II, p. 123.

[46]_OR_, pt. II, pp. 382,438.

[47]_OR_, pt. I, p. 862.

[48]_OR_, pt. II, p. 30; Milo M. Quaife, ed., _From the

Cannon's Mouth, the Civil War Letters of General Alpheus S._

Williams (Detroit: Wayne State University Press, 1959), p. 312;

Jack K. Bauer, ed., *Soldiering, the Civil War Diary of Rice C. Bull*

(Novato: Presidio Press, 1995), p. 116.

[49]*Atlanta Papers*, p. 79

[50]*OR*, pt. III, pp. 813,818,833.

[51]*OR*, pt. III, pp. 818,843,855.

[52]*OR*, pt. II, p. 123.

[53]*From the Cannon's Mouth*, p. 312; *OR*, pt. II, p. 123.

[54]"William A. Brown's Book," December 21, 1867, mss. at
Kennesaw Mountain National Battlefield Park, p. 166

[55]Julian Wisner Hinkley, *A Narrative of Service With the
3rd Wisconsin Infantry* (Wisconsin History Commission, 1912), p.
122; *OR*, pt. II, p. 30.

[56]Samuel H. Hurst, *Journal-History of the 73rd Ohio
Volunteer Infantry* (Chillicothe, 1866), p. 127.

[57]*OR*, pt. II, p. 382.

[58]S. F. Fleharty, *Our Regiment, A History of the 102d
Illinois Infantry Volunteers* (Chicago: Brewster and Hanscom,
1865), p. 69.

[59]OR, pt. II, pp. 342-343.

[60]OR, pt. II, pp. 123,279; *From the Cannon's Mouth*, p. 313.

[61]OR, pt. II, pp. 124,167,264,396,438; Stone,79. It is interesting to note that none of the Confederate battle reports mention the storm.

[62]*Soldiering*, pp. 117-118.

[63]Howard in *Battles and Leaders*, vol.4, pp. 306-307.

[64]Clyde C. Walton, ed., *Private Smith's Journal, Recollections of the Late War* (Chicago: Lakeside Press, 1963), pp. 151-152.

[65]J. A. Payne, "In Light Vein," in *Confederate Veteran* (vol. 38, #6, June 1930), p.246.

[66]OR, pt. II, pp. 14,30,125,324. Casualties include killed, wounded, and missing. There is a discrepancy, however, between the losses reported by Hooker and those of his divisional commanders. In his OR report Williams counted 745 casualties, Butterfield 268, and Geary 509, for a total of 1522. This tally more accurately reflects the participation by Geary's

and Butterfield's divisions: Geary played a major role in both phases of the battle, while Butterfield was engaged only in the second phase, with one of his brigades seeing little action therein.

[67]*OR*, pt. III, pp. 616,818.

[68]*Soldiering*, p. 119.

[69]*A Southern Boy in Blue*, pp. 289-290.

[70]Jacob D. Cox, *Sherman's Battle for Atlanta* (New York: Da Capo Press, 1994), p. 75.

[71]*Sherman's Civil War*, p. 655.

[72]*OR*, pt. IV, p. 312.

[73]Sherman, *Memoirs*, p. 45.

[74]*Rough Side of War*, pp. 212-213.

[75]Sherman, *Memoirs*, p. 44, emphasis added.

[76]*Soldiering*, pp. 121-122.

[77]*OR*, pt. III, pp. 705,761.

[78]*OR*, pt. I, p. 193,294; pt. II, pp. 124,207,383.

[79]*OR*, pt. II, pp. 567,680,766. Hovey's Division was detached; see p. 18.

---

[80]OR, pt. I, p. 144; pt. IV, pp. 324,386. While operating southwest of Atlanta, General Palmer, commanding the 14th Corps, was ordered to cooperate with Schofield, Army of the Ohio commander. Palmer refused to obey Schofield's orders, contending that Schofield was junior to him. An order from Sherman supporting Schofield did not change anything, except to prompt Palmer's second resignation. After attempts by Sherman and Thomas to mollify Palmer failed, the resignation was accepted.

[81]OR, pt. III, pp. 34,95,379-380.

[82]OR, pt. IV, p. 32.

[83] referred to by Union commanders as the "North Marietta Road", and labeled the "Dallas-Acworth Road" on the map

[84]OR, pt. IV, p. 323.

[85]OR, pt. IV, p. 327.

[86]OR, pt. I, p. 194.

[87]OR, pt. IV, p. 327.

[88]William B. Hazen, A Narrative of   Military Service (Boston, 1885), p.276.

[89]OR, pt. I, pp. 561, 594. R.M.Collins, *Chapters from the Unwritten History of the War Between the States* (Dayton, 1988), p.209.   C.C.Briant, *History of the Sixth Regiment, Indiana Volunteer Infantry* (Indianapolis: 1891), p.316.

[90]OR, pt.1,p.379.

[91]W.W.Mackall, *A Son's Recollections of His Father* (New York, 1930), p.211.

[92]OR,pt.1, p. 193-194; pt.2, p.680; pt.4, p.325; Cox, *Atlanta*, p.77.

[93]John B. Hood, *Advance and Retreat* (Secuacus, 1985.), p. 119.

[94]OR, pt.3, p. 724.

[95]OR, pt.1, p. 377.

[96]Robert L.Kimberly and Ephraim S. Holloway, *The Forty-First Ohio Veteran Volunteer Infantry in the War of the Rebellion. 1861-1865.* (Cleveland, 1897), pp. 83-84.

[97]OR, pt.1, pp.194, 377.

[98]OR, pt.4, p.324.

[99]OR, pt.1, p.377.

[100]Hazen, *Narrative*, p.257.

[101]Bierce, "The Crime at Pickett's Mill", p. 41.

[102]*OR*, pt.1, p.   194; pt.2, p. 680.

[103]Bierce, "Crime", p. 42.

[104]*OR*, pt.1, p. 377.

[105]*OR*, pt.3, pp.724-725.

[106]Collins, *Chapters*, p.211.

[107]*OR*, pt.3, pp.724-725.

[108]Hood, *Advance and Retreat*, p.117.

[109]Bierce, "Crime," p. 44.

[110]*OR*, pt.3, p.725.

[111]Hazen, *Narrative*, p.257.

[112]*OR*, pt.1, p.423.

[113]*OR*, pt.1, pp.194-195.

[114]*OR*, pt.3, p.725.

[115] Briant, *History*, pp. 319-320

[116]Hazen, *Narrative*, p.258.

[117]*OR*, pt.3, p.725.

[118]General M.P. Lowrey, "General M.P. Lowrey,   An

Autobiography", *Southern Historical Society Papers*, Vol.16 (Richmond:1876-).

[119]Cox, *Atlanta*, p.79.

[120]*OR*,   pt.1, p.595.

[121]*OR*, pt.1, p.442.

[122]Bierce, "Crime", p. 48.

[123]Silas Crowell, "The General Wept", in "The National Tribune", December 31, 1896.

[124]*OR*, pt.1, p.424.

[125]*OR*, pt.1, p.378.

[126]*OR*, pt.1, p.378.

[127]*OR*, pt. 1, pp. 413-414.

[128]*OR*, pt.1, p.387; Andrew J. Gleason, "Confusion as to Names," in "The National Tribune," February 11, 1897.

[129]*OR*, pt.1,   pp.865-866.

[130]*OR*, pt.1,   p.447.

[131]*OR*, pt.1,   p.595.

[132]*OR*, pt.1, p.448.

[133]*OR*,   pt.3, p.725.

[134]Collins, *Chapters*, p. 214.

[135]*OR*, pt.3, p.726.

[136]*OR*, pt.1, p.379.

[137]Norman D. Brown, ed. *One of Cleburne's Command, The Civi War Reminiscences and Diary of Capt. Samuel T. Foster, Granbury's Texas Brigade, CSA* (Austin, 1980), p.85.

[138]*OR*, pt.1, p.595.

[139]G.W.Lewis, *The Campaigns of the 124th Regiment Ohio Volunteer Infantry* (Akron, 1894), p.152.

[140]Frederick C. Cross, ed. *Nobly They Served the Union* (Frederick C. Cross, 1976), p.88.

[141]Collins, *Chapters*, p 215.

[142]Brown, *One of Cleburne's Command*, p.88.

[143]Collins, *Chapters*, p.215.

[144]Henry Fales Perry, *History of the Thirty-Eighth Regiment, Indiana Volunteer Infantry, One of the Three Hundred Fighting Regiments of the Union Army in the War of the Rebellion, 1861-1865* (Palo Alto, 1906), p.138.

[145]*OR*, pt.3, p. 726.

[146]Bierce, "Crime," p. 49.

[147]Study by author based on casualty reports in *OR*.

[148]*Battles & Leaders*, IV, 308; B. F. Scribner, *How Soldiers Were Made* (Huntington, WV, 1995), p. 247.

[149]Cox, *Atlanta*, pp.79-80.

[150]*OR*, pt.3, p.677, 726, 987.

[151]Cox, *Atlanta*, p.80.

[152]*OR*, pt.1, pp.523, 527.

[153]*OR*, pt.1, p.867.

[154]*OR*, pt. IV, pp. 331,333.

[155]*OR*, pt. IV, p. 331.

[156]Sherman, *Memoirs*, p. 45.

[157]*OR*, pt. IV, p. 336. On the "Dallas Line, May 27" map, this road is labeled "Dallas-Acworth Rd". McCook's position is to the east of the map-view.

[158]*OR*, pt. I, pp. 630,679,710.

[159]*OR*, pt. III, pp. 130, 380.

[160]*OR*, pt. III, p. 264; *Diary of a Confederate Soldier*, p. 133.

[161]OR, pt. III, p. 95.

[162]OR, pt. III, p. 95.

[163]OR, pt. III, p. 706.

[164]OR, pt. III, p. 153; Savas, The Campaign for Atlanta, pp. 209-210.

[165]W. J. McMurray, M.D. History of the Twentieth Tennessee Regiment Infantry, CSA (Nashville: The Publication Committee, 1904), p. 313.

[166]Strayer, Larry M. and Baumgartner, Richard A. Echoes of Battle (Huntington: Blue Acorn Press, 1991), p. 127.

[167]OR, pt. III, pp. 315-316.

[168]Savas,vol.1, p. 210; OR, pt. III, p. 706.

[169]Savas, p. 210; Johnston, Narrative, p. 332; OR, pt. IV, p. 343. It is also significant that on the same day Johnston asked Major General Lovell, a volunteer on his staff, to "examine the fords and ferries of the Chattahoochee [River]" in order to protect them from Federal cavalry raids. However, it may also have been a preliminary action to an expected withdrawal.

[170]Savas, pp. 210-211.

[171]Savas, pp. 210-211.

[172]Jackman, p. 132.

[173]*OR*, pt. III, p. 687; Kirwan, *Johnny Green*, p.133.

[174]*OR*, pt. III, pp. 145-146.

[175]Strayer and Baumgartner, pp. 126,128; *OR*, pt. III, pp. 131,145,162.

[176]*OR*, pt. III, p. 96; Simpson & Berlin, eds. *Sherman's Civil War*, p. 644.

[177]Letter, "Headquarters 2nd Div. 15th A. C. Dallas, Georgia, May 29, 1864", Thomas Thomson Taylor Papers, Emory University Special Collections, Atlanta, Ga.

[178]*OR*, pt. III, p. 303.

[179]*OR*, pt. III, p. 95.

[180]*OR*, pt. III, pp. 96,687; Savas,215.

[181]Savas, p. 213; Kirwan, p. 133; *OR*, pt. III, p. 989.

[182]*OR*, pt. IV, pp. 339-340.

[183]Kirwan, p. 134; Savas, pp. 214-215.

[184]Jackman, pp. 133-134.

[185]Buck, Irving A., Captain, *Cleburne and His Command*, edited by T. R. Hay (Wilmington: Broadfoot Publishing Co., 222.

[186]*OR*, pt. III, pp. 215,380,404.

[187]Kirwan, p. 134.

[188]Johnston, pp. 333-334; *Battles & Leaders*, vol. IV, p. 270.

[189]Hood, *Advance*, pp. 120-121. Little Pumkinvine Creek was also called Pickett's Mill Creek, the site of the battle May 27.

[190]*OR*, pt. I, pp. 529,596.

[191]*OR*, pt. III, p. 987.

[192]*OR*, pt. III, pp. 874-875.

[193]Puntenney, Sgt. George H. *History of the Thirty-Seventh Regiment of Indiana Infantry Volunteers* (Rushville: Jacksonian Book and Job Dept, 1896), p. 96.

[194]*OR*, pt. IV, p. 343.

[195]*OR*, pt. IV, p. 385.

[196]Sherman, *Memoirs*, p. 46.

[197]OR, pt. III, pp. 707,990.

[198]Jackman, p. 135. "The night of the 29th May" refers to the "Lightning Bug Battle".

[199]Bull, *Soldiering*, p. 121-122.

[200]OR, pt. III, pp. 707,716,991.

[201]OR, pt. II, p. 681.

[202]OR, pt. II, p. 512.

[203]OR, pt. II, pp. 512,542.

[204]Johnston, p. 335.

[205]Sherman, *Memoirs*, p. 46; *Sherman's Civil War*, p. 643.

[206]OR, pt. III, p. 687; Sherman, *Memoirs*, p. 48.

[207]*Memoirs*, p. 49.

Works Cited

Bauer, Jack K., ed. *Soldiering, the Civil War Diary of
    Rice C. Bull.* Novato, California: Presidio Press,
    1995.

Bierce, Ambrose, "The Crime at Pickett's Mill," *Ambrose
    Bierce's Civil War.* Washington, D.C.: Regnery
    Gateway, 1956.

Briant, C. C. *History of the Sixth Regiment, Indiana
    Volunteer Infantry.* Indianapolis, Indiana: W. B.
    Burford, Printer and Binders, 1891.

Brown, Norman D., ed. *One of Cleburne's Command,
    The Civi War Reminiscences and Diary of Capt.
    Samuel T. Foster, Granbury's Texas Brigade, CSA.*
    Austin, Texas, 1980.

Charles Harding Cox Papers. Letter from "Near
    Altoona, Ga., May 24th, 1864". Atlanta, Georgia:
    Emory University Special Collections.

Collins, R.M. *Chapters from the Unwritten History of the
    War Between the States.* Dayton, Ohio:
    Morningside Press, 1988.

Cox, Jacob D. *Sherman's Battle for Atlanta.* New York:
    Da Capo Press, 1994.

Cross, Frederick C., ed. *Nobly They Served the Union.*
    Frederick C. Cross, 1976.

Davis, William C., ed. *Diary of a Confederate Soldier,
   John S. Jackman of the Orphan Brigade.*
   Columbia, South Carolina: University of South
   Carolina Press, 1990.

Fleharty, S. F. *Our Regiment, A History of the 102d
   Illinois Infantry Volunteers.* Chicago, Illinois:
   Brewster and Hanscom, 1865.

Gates, Arnold, ed. *The Rough Side of War: The Civil War
   Journal of Chesley Mosman.* Garden City, New
   York: Basin Publishing Co., 1987.

Hay, T. R., ed. *Cleburne and His Command by Captain
   Irving A. Buck.* Wilmington, North Carolina:
   Broadfoot Publishing Co., 1995.

Hazen, William B. *A Narrative of Military Service.*
   Boston, Massachusetts: Ticknor & Co., 1885.

Hinkley, Julian Wisner. *A Narrative of Service With the
   3rd Wisconsin Infantry.* Wisconsin History
   Commission, 1912.

Hood, John B. *Advance and Retreat.* Secuacus, New
   Jersey, 1985.

Howard, O. O. "The Struggle for Atlanta," in *Battles and
   Leaders of the Civil War*, vol. IV. Secaucus, New
   Jersey: Castle, 1982.

Hurst, Samuel H. *Journal-History of the 73rd Ohio
   Volunteer Infantry.* Chillicothe, Ohio, 1866.

Johnston, Joseph E. *Narrative of Military Operations
   During the Civil War.* New York: Da Capo Press,
   1959.

Kerksis, Sydney C., ed. *The Atlanta Papers.* Dayton,
   Ohio: Morningside Bookshop Press, 1980.

Kimberly, Robert L. and Holloway, Ephraim S. *The
   Forty-First Ohio Veteran Volunteer Infantry in the
   War of the Rebellion. 1861-1865.* Cleveland,
   Ohio, 1897.

Kirwan, A. D., ed. *Johnny Green of the Orphan Brigade,
   A Journal of a Confederate Soldier.* Lexington,
   Kentucky: University of Kentucky Press, 1956.

Lewis, G. W. *The Campaigns of the 124th Regiment Ohio Volunteer Infantry*. Akron, Ohio: Werner Co., 1894.

Lowrey, M. P. "General M. P. Lowrey, An Autobiography", *Southern Historical Society Papers*, Vol.16 (1876-).

Mackall, W. W. *A Son's Recollections of His Father*. New York, 1930.

McMurray, W. J., M.D. *History of the Twentieth Tennessee Regiment Infantry, CSA*. Nashville, Tennessee: The Publication Committee, 1904.

Newton, Steven H. "Formidable Only in a Fight?" *North and South Magazine*, Vol.3, #4.

Noe, Kenneth W., ed. *A Southern Boy in Blue: The Memoir of Marcus Woodcock, 9th Kentucky Infantry*. Knoxville, Tennessee: University of Tennessee Press, 1996.

Payne, J. A. "In Light Vein". *Confederate Veteran*, Vol. 38, #6 (June 1930).

Perry, Henry Fales. *History of the Thirty-Eighth Regiment, Indiana Volunteer Infantry, One of the Three Hundred Fighting Regiments of the Union Army in the War of the Rebellion, 1861-1865*. Palo Alto, California, 1906.

Puntenney, Sgt. George H. *History of the Thirty-Seventh Regiment of Indiana Infantry Volunteers*. Rushville: Jacksonian Book and Job Dept., 1896.

Quaife, Milo M., ed. *From the Cannon's Mouth, the Civil War Letters of General Alpheus S. Williams*. Detroit, Michigan: Wayne State University Press, 1959.

Scaife, William R. *The Campaign for Atlanta*. Cartersville, Georgia: Civil War Publications, 1993.

Scribner, B. F. *How Soldiers Were Made*. Huntington, West Virginia: Blue Acorn Press, 1995.

Sherman, William T. *Memoirs of General William T.
    Sherman, By Himself,* Vol. II. Indiana University
    Press, Civil War Centennial Series, 1957.

Simpson, Brooks D. and Berlin, Jean V., ed. *Sherman's
    Civil War, Selected Correspondence of William T.
    Sherman, 1860-1865.* Chapel Hill: University of
    North Carolina Press, 1999.

Thomas Thomson Taylor Papers. Letter, "Headquarters
    2nd Div. 15th A. C. Dallas, Georgia, May 29,
    1864". Atlanta, Georgia, Emory University
    Special Collections.

U. S. War Department. *The War of the Rebellion: A
    Compilation of the Official Records of the Union
    and Confederate Armies.* 128 vols. Washington:
    Government Printing Office, 1880-1901.

Walton, Clyde C., ed. *Private Smith's Journal,
    Recollections of the Late War* Chicago, Illinois:
    Lakeside Press, 1963.

Waters, Zack C., ed. "The Partial Atlanta Reports of
    Confederate Maj. Gen. William B. Bate," in
    Savas, Theodore P. and Woodbury, David A., ed.
    The Campaign for Atlanta, vol. I. Campbell,
    California: Savas Woodbury Publishers, 1994.

"William A. Brown's Book," December 21, 1867, mss.
    Kennesaw Mountain National Battlefield Park

Index

14th Corps, vi, 5, 9, 10, 16, 30, 36, 37, 40, 88, 116
20th Corps, 5, 6, 9, 15, 16, 34
4th Corps, 5, 10, 19, 36, 39, 40
Dallas
  Georgia, 1, 2, 8, 9, 10, 11, 12, 15, 16, 17, 19, 20, 31, 33, 35, 36, 37, 38, 39, 42, 69, 73, 74, 75, 77, 84, 85, 91, 92, 95
Dallas Line, iv, vi, 33, 37, 84, 92, 94, 97, 98
Davis, Jefferson C., v, 1, 2, 10, 36, 37, 38, 70, 71
Dodge, Grenville, 6, 15, 36, 38, 86
Eldridge, John W., 23, 30
Etowah River, v, vi, 1, 2, 5, 6, 7, 8, 9, 10, 11, 99
Florida Troops
  Finley's Brigade, 12, 85
French, Samuel G., 29
Garrard, Kenner, 6, 11, 15, 37, 91

Geary, John, 9, 10, 16, 17, 18, 19, 20, 23, 24, 25, 27, 29, 31, 35, 36
Grant, Ulysses S., iii, iv, v, 31
Hardee, William, 11, 12, 16, 35, 39, 42, 71, 87, 91, 93
Harrow, William, 15, 71, 73, 81, 82, 83
Hascall, Milo, 9, 10, 15, 36, 93, 94
Hell Hole, iv, 32, 33, 41, 64
Hindman, Thomas, 23, 35, 42, 61, 66, 90
Hooker, Joseph, 5, 6, 7, 9, 10, 15, 16, 18, 19, 20, 24, 26, 29, 31, 32, 35, 36, 37, 38, 39, 70, 71, 91, 93, 94
Hotchkiss, T. R., 42, 49
Hovey, Alvin, vi, 10, 15, 93, 94
Howard, Oliver Otis, 5, 19, 20, 28, 30, 32, 36, 38, 39, 40, 45, 46, 47, 52, 55, 57, 59, 62, 64, 65, 66, 67, 68, 70, 87
Illinois Troops
  103rd Infantry, 74, 82
  1st Artillery, 71

www.ingramcontent.com/pod-product-compliance
Lightning Source LLC
Chambersburg PA
CBHW060356090426
42734CB00011B/2146